Lisa Fannen is a vital, new voice in Bri
stand where the tectonic plates of inter
registering those seismic shocks – and
worlds, the vision and artistry to powe
vidual and collective transformation.

Faultline is richly diverse, with poems drawing on acute observ… personal experiences in the UK and US (including bereavement and work at a herbal foot clinic on Skid Row), which are interwoven with other important political poems, many meticulously researched and written in response to events of national and global significance, such as the Hillsborough Final Inquest Verdict and the Fukushima nuclear disaster.

This is wild, raw poetry, words bristling off the page with righteous anger against oppression and as satire of the neoliberal capitalist system, juxtaposed with exquisite moments of grief, tender connection, insight. Lisa Fannen's debut collection deserves attention, as it promises to become a cherished companion for anyone trying to survive within the crazy-making system we're simultaneously attempting to change.

— Helen Moore, www.helenmoorepoet.com

Fannen's work is a siren call, a blessing, a whisper. Socially and politically aware, Fannen's words offer up a vibrating tremor of language, daring us to be fully alive and feel. She delivers words/syntax in a volley of compassion and consideration. Fannen topsy turvey's poetics and bears witness to the layerings of life. She takes you to the Faultline, holds your hand and gently, makes you look.

— Raman Mundair

The common thread running through these poems is that of kindness. Lisa sees with a kind eye, reacts with a kind mind and then, like the person on the night train 'pulling the trolley backwards', dispenses that kindness with considered gentleness; tea, biscuits and, in Lisa's case, a healthy dose of poetry. Ah, that's better. Here are the completely un-cynical reactions of a good person to what might to others be perceived as a bad world. The message is clear; it is we who make the world around us, so do something about it, or, in Lisa's own words, 'bare yourself; be generous'.

— Penny Rimbaud

što čitaš?

First printing
Donji Budački, Croatia
October 2018

ISBN 9781909798595

www.activedistribution.org
www.stocitas.org

Faultline

Lisa Fannen

For my father Anthony Fannen
(1929 - 2014)
With thanks

Faultline

Affirmation # 6
Believe the best is yet to come

She was sailing   in a big bowl

then a bucket   and then a boat

She mouthed something to you   then said

she would take your child   to safety

and come back for you too   clinging

from a tree   or on a roof top

or up to your knees   in brown mud

You open your eyes   it's still dark

Minion

This thundering volume
people tight in the economy
carving out career paths, selling their skin
bound like wire, heart race, heat and 11 hour days.

The bird flight beneath the bridge, a gull
the huge swollen Thames tide licking at the steps
I catch the occasional sky, glance up
look
see
Venus is still there.

It's young men mostly
tired eyes
raking from the filthy streets
commission
of other people's insubstantial shelter.

Lungs undone, the air in between the chase
of the road and the coming night time
holding bunches of keys at the steering wheel

> You slam the car door
> you have a new coat
> you say to yourself that
> your job is never the same thing every day
> you like working with people
> you like working out and about
> that I can contact you on your mobile
> from 8 am til 9 at night.

We see, flat viewing —
a picture frame, family photos, kitchen things
plasma TV, a drinks shelf, different shaped glasses.

Next — one family in 2 box rooms
3 toddlers (small shoes lined up in the bedroom)
close up to the TV

and the landlord arriving
just as we are leaving.

Everybody owns nobody owns anything
people the world over
hocking their teeth to pay the rent
the market cushioned in casual clothes here.

The land and life that is stolen
and sold back.

That you are a seller.

Step out of the car
the children are clapping
the children are clapping and singing
bags on their backs
all their lives ahead of them.

Knowledge Rooms

I revolve into a foyer the size of a car lot
just two leather sofas, the ceiling abbey above
a reception desk as long as a cocktail bar.

In this glass palace one silent elevator winds
up and down, doors slide mute transportation
people step into the building, shed overcoats
hear their own footsteps echo — their stride
facilitated in the acres of permission.

I've come to cover someone's class —
too late in the day to cancel, my eyes scan
google search, my heart sinking from its ligament
cradle between sternum & spine;

Sustainability, shale gas...

The double-speak like a sewerage sluice
guising pages for the nuclear industry
and pipeline construction, pinkwashed
with the Stonewall Equality Index:
Top 100 Employers 2017.

Seems the IRA bombing, early 90s, didn't disable
this legal force, it just licked its blast wounds
of brickdust and wire and forged on —
security guards chaperone now
at the building mouth.

The class is in K1. Heavy doored suites
called 'Knowledge Rooms' housing
coffee machines, long fluted glasses.

Two older women from payroll uncurl their mats
two young lawyers lie back, release
we trace bones, vertebra by vertebra
the shape of stories so far — bills to pay

raising teenagers or just out of law school
the relentless pressures of aspiration
backs held, smelted and angled.

We make a tenderness together
a momentary rest, even in this place
the breath that is between us.

I step out
it's dark —
young solicitors
chewing at prepacked sandwiches
are staying late, eyes melted into screen glare
on all floors.

London Bridge is Falling Down

God would tell me George, go and fight those terrorists
in Afghanistan, and I did, and then God would tell me George,
go end the tyranny in Iraq, and I did.
— George W. Bush

The summer rain sweetening the city.
Through the fine mist Ramadan peacefully
laddering musical scales from inside the Mosque.

Striplit the sun is sinking.
Twilight the traffic peeling over the damp concrete.
The call to prayer offering pause in its hands
breaking fast.

The arc of low pressure bars —
it's a hanging warm the weekend is swelling into.

*

Like worms after the rain all of London has come up to the
surface.
The subways have been shut. Cars standstill. Huge crowds trail
the streets in mobile glow trying to get places, cross the river.

At 11.17pm the bridge is closed.
I cannot get into my street.
Journalists pressure anyone walking from behind the lines for
copy
and the police woman, finally her chance to enact, off the dull
beat
cannot wait to tell me this is now a *sterile zone*.

The helicopter snarls, tilting loops of 8, exhausting the sky.
Beneath, this global north marks itself safe on facebook
(conversation closer)
it being blinkers *and* bridle.

Scotland Yard announces an
unprecendented
50 rounds to shoot the three men dead.

The media salivates over eyewitness accounts
claiming the attackers had said this
This is for Allah.

Southwark Cathedral

The pipes open full
shock to the stone foundations
strange in the muted not response dancing
you aren't allowed to anything   clap
let out your own sound   strength

The pipes open, the ecstatic contradiction
the soul enlivened/the spirit restrained
asks where is pagan heritage
to power among and
sat under the organ I wonder —
who carved the wood, who turned the metal
who bonded the leather, cut the keys?

The pipes fluted, soft
the pipes shuddering
blood rush
here on the stolen ground —
under the stone slabs an old temple
under the stone slabs and temple, wood
under the stone slabs, temple and wood, earth
in the earth the remains of a well

The recital sheet requests
donations in the nave by the font
and I think
women selling their bodies in Southwark stews
paid enough tax to the Bishop of Winchester here
the Church, a wealthy enough corporation
century by century the land and people bled

The final outpouring
that holding note
and holding
like you might stay forever in
the wild chord resonating

Then it ends
the muffled sound of the stops going back in
wooden, closing

Outside the bus brakes
wheel axle of a train passing
the drilling into the pavement

Layerings on the Lambeth Road

1263
Commons

Low lying marshes
Red Kites, yellow dandelions, but of a winter
nothing, nothing but bleak mids and hard as iron;

1672
The Dog and Duck

The spa 'purging waters', the tavern
and the duck baiting pond
the license revoke and stories
whores, rogues and highwaymen;

1799
School for the Indigent Blind

Of Blake's lambs here 15 women and men
feeling around wooden handrails in the darkness
in receipt of instruction of trades for subsistence;

1815
Bedlam

How they held a competition; a grand design
a great poverty to house the unruly and anyone else
speaking with the Angels;

1934
Geraldine Mary Harmsworth Park

The park gifted to the splendid
struggling mothers of Southwark;

1936
The Imperial War museum

Display cabinets
The blood that never dried
Dalai Lama in the Tibetan peace garden
That chunk of the Berlin wall
next to the Naval guns that says
Change your life;

Home

Edged in, the city's compression
a contraction at the diaphragm
I tread small pilgrimages
seek the old wells and springs
the high hill, the heath and rivers
culverted beneath the streets
I lean in, try to hear the Fleet
running under the grating
at the Farringdon crossroads.

I beat the bounds, way marking
and they made great procession
field edge and parish stone
with birch switches and willow boughs
wandering from hawthorn to hazel
in Dickens Square Park
honouring the holly at the railing
on Harper Road.

I step out to turn in, and just sit —
listen to the poplars
speaking the wind from the coast
passing through and away out again
trading us breath.

This space as salvage —
I faint back into woodpeckers
that come laughing quiet Sundays
blackbird, wren and the foxes den
warm fur, just out the back
buffered from the main drag
by the Crown Court walls.

This is no time for order
the undoing mind —
everything you filled up
small self, fall away —

that which won’t
come from you
list-ticker
but enters the loose realms.

It is right here holy place
right here home —
 this conurbation just
 guest settlement
 in the territory.

Sunset — face up in praise
the solar fire lowering in solitary bliss
and the night to know
even for the street lights
I open to call the planets as family
the Moon burnt amber
Jupiter powering its white sphere
the centres of gravitational massive
and centuries of pull and swing above
the swollen river at London Bridge.
And later, the tide racing out
over the Southbank beaches
coming back up again for air.

The Apple Store

This fawning over thin things svelte, glowing, the hyper colour
real-world-beauty to flick at, what's the verb for that motion
moving things on a touch screen with your fingers?

The shimmering mirage in this temple to the age of more and more
born by young hands dulled over the motherboards of this endless
consumption; shaving the aluminium off the edge of the apple logo
they strung suicide nets up after 9 jumps in the space of 3 months

Shenzhen
Guangdong province
north of Hong Kong
where

manufactured poverty assembles the fetish that
pretty young things can sling in a bag — so free, so easy
media making, spirit breaking, collapsing of the deep soul into a
race
for new models Microsoft, Dell, Hewlett Packard and on and on
nausea and on and on and on:

93 million iphones
40 million ipads
38 million ipods
17 million computers

in one year

Here, bound in to long working hours and electrical hum
sales team techies are saying the same things over —
RAM memory processors

I can't tell you
this empty sorrow

the heavy drag for how the joy could be,
unfettered by this show of loss.

Blood test

Here we are this airless tower
airless and vacuum, the forces
made mute at the doorways and the windows
the spirits make it in
on the soles of our shoes, soil, maybe
in the occasional song.

Fourth floor funnel
the corridors twist and corner
old lino, the plastic seating that
scrapes on the flooring making marks
the blue walls, all those litres and litres of paint.

Everybody's arm outstretched on the same
cushioning, a piece of withered couch-roll
unchanged between elbows
the tie of the tourniquet
the readying vein.

The LED summons, the call
that comes from behind the curtain
and back to back the sound
of glass vials filling, O and AO
attached, collecting, falling into trays.

We go in
one after the other after another
pale nurse breaking out needle after needle
drawing and drawing, sealing plastic lab bags

arm after arm
vein after vein
tiny strip lit cubicle.

It's something specific sickness, sickly this
particular over and over, this particular
again and again
hour after hour.

Routes Out

I am leaving the buildings
their thick relational cluster;
mono-species piled on top of each other
the street lattice and cars and car air
and the hard racing roads.

I'm taking a route out east to the marshes
the pylons there pin-bolts in the landscape
leashing the earth with voltage, beneath
the elderberries lie dark purple crush
in the gravel path, the wind bevelling
the water that gently pulses reeds, lilies
a plastic bag, a tennis ball.

It's a strange portal: canal, cables, reservoirs
its own peace though the corridor is at odds
with wilderness —
nature reserves, plaques and signposts
a container to free from yet.

The city's edge teases between tree lines
rubble heaps, process plants, gas cylinders
a train whines on a track, the heat of the sun
opens my pores then there is the cool
contraction of cloud cover.

Eventually it's sweet and green
all noise has folded away behind
I stop and lean on a wooden gate
listen to the quiet expanding

Para ceta mol

What's the half life of your hours
undigested, propping yourself up
at the bus stop in the rain, running
late again, metal foil against a filling

small
compact

Someone has marketed caplets
and child's doses to swallow
barcode
and on the side of the packet

for the relief of mild to moderate pain

A room in a house
the bed covers back
the fire out

Your gentleness

Is this what you will do
for how long
with your gentleness

Squeezing the hot water
on the tea trolley
with your gentleness

Pulling the trolley backwards
saying *hi George*,
nobody buying much this time of night train
with your gentleness

Counting out the change
soft eyes and push your glasses
up your nose again after they slip forward
from looking down
with your gentleness

Will you be a long time here
doing this,
later you passing with a clear bag for rubbish
with your gentleness

Chance encounter

I left the baking city
the train plunging into thick sea fog
and at the end of the line, no brakes
slipping chain, rode the perimeter fence
that marks the land stolen
from the shoreline
          forbidden
in blue print

Weekend permitted
the barriers raised
          stick to the path
          spent shells or munitions
          to be left unhandled
between the firing ranges
everywhere was hawthorn and
everywhere it was all in flower

I made it to the Wakering Stairs
where the sea pulls away for miles
seeping over the mudflats, then
the coast path that bends to Southend
where the weekend had swollen in
small town, the front smelling
of chip fat and sugar

It was busy, people taking
rides under bassy speakers
and flashing lights the colour
of boiled sweets

I walked the pier, a mile and a quarter
stretching into the mist, just the sound
of those wooden boards over the waves
that were deep and deepening

Made a chance encounter
by the cafeteria where the skeleton

ceases and there's only water rocking
at its frame — man from Colombia
who had run the length of the pier out
and, inspired, I readied myself
to join him running it back

Effortless in his skin, soft pacing
light in his steps he made easy
conversation even as I had to dig in
thinking — the land in sight —
I might not make it

Our ending, pleased beaming
a brief farewell, an embrace —
his photo of me staggering
to the finish, he tripped off
still running, disappeared
into the promenade crowds
calling back

You know —
you have to do something
to remember each day by

In the Embrace

The clock that is killing us
that is driving us all asunder
School runs and rush hours
mullen mouthpieces
race and racing.

Lunch break and us locked
in conversation headlights —
all Question/Answer, a nervous tick
gritted-smiling in that talk-snare
while the heart cloaks itself
against the barren territory.

Tears strike upwards —
the shock of slowing to sensation again
all the unfelt of daily steel and slate
and in those after hours
everything on the outside

laugh like a hyena
grimace in the right places
fingering text messages
hello hello at the bar

Nervous normal no room
a velocity speak keeping us apart
nothing spirit or space emergent
had a little drink about an hour ago
miming happy like you haven't just pulled
through five days data-entry so your landlord
can holiday in the Algarve. Again.

In the embrace, warmth, tenderness
dissolving into woodland, no alarm division
weekdays and weekends, only the heat of the sun
then the sun going, only the praying heart
the things that need done, you stop when you tire
or need to eat, or when the daylight closes.

This pace within the body us all turning
in the great coherent wheel
residing in the magical
not levered out industrial discipline —
how the iron tracks came bringing timetables
unhinging the sundials, pulling us out
of the realm of the sensory.

Let’s pick apart the mechanics
the small coil and glass casing in pieces on the table
the long and the short hand
take the sand out of the hourglass.

We might fall through salt tides and run on the hill
                              laid down our defences
our temporary bones how they will ground
not the rapid, halted breath, high in the chest
too many days at schedule
steering us away.

Forced Swim Test

O small ones
four small feet —
snacking on barbiturates
monoamine breakfasts
amphetamines before bed.

They lift you by the tails
lower you into the tank
the crazed marker
set standard —
the Forced Swim Test.

You swim and you swim
on your diet of stimulants, no
elimination of hopelessness; just
lights, cameras, stop watches
monitoring your determination
panic, right to the last
of near exhausted success.

You beat the clock.
Result.
Mobility and float.
They warm you on heat pads.
Return you to cages.

Findings are listed in lists
this to make happiness-sales
in variable profits, on the back
of all that waterlogged fur
sunk, and rolling in abandon
at the base of clear glass jars.

Sleep Cycle

1. Darkness

The beds are full & overflowing
          sleepless & adrenal

supine & prostrate —
accident   and emergency

drenched in blue light
glued to screens

it's been suggested tinted lenses
would be the cheapest option

It is your loss but
you can imagine

the traces remain
gather them

you heard it on the wind
now it speaks to you

Break the circuitry addict
go under —

Wrap yourself in the darkness
let it be dark behind your eyelids
a granite boulder on your diaphragm
vision come come story —

Lie still

Let the night

2. Second sleep

The colour drains out of the day
the tallow flame darts, flickers, the wick burns out
smokes, close bodies settle back, minds folding in
breath falling heavy and rhythmic
eyes swimming like fish under eyelids

Dreams acquire structure, the kaleidoscope
of the days inner workings reveal themselves
the quiet hours   they open porous

In the midnight silence people emerge
depth to surface; the cobbler in the frozen winter
stoking the fire, women of the cloth making recitations
night vigils while children reach for mouthfuls
of bread and warm beer

And in the watch skin finding skin
and in the thick summer rising to visit neighbours
the roll of die, candle fire licking round bowls of fat
casting shadows, then the wending return, alleys
doorways, back under bedclothes, all lanolin weight
on mattresses stuffed with mugwort
dropping into slumber again
diving down

*

The city hums three blocks away, I wake
trace my spirit home, this peaceable hour
undone the aggravated strain of the day
loosed of the armouring premise of rationalism
scrabbling to explain-fix, limbed off components
in the bind of cause-and-effect logic

It's cool here
It's cool here and widening
bathing the nerve fibres, travelling through the tissues
making their song low, lulling their pulse to a slow, elastic

refrain, the fall of rain on the empty street outside
playing to this ancestral pattern
deep in the lymph and the marrow

*

Listen to the talk, squinting at human history
through bottle lenses, speaking word-splinters:
bi-modal rhythms it is speculated (then assimilated)
useful for *stress*
management, how the magical is accumulated
and collapse it into the flat functional
of industrial modernity —

the pineal gland it is said
this wakefulness an endocrinology all of its own

is the calm habitat, the open soul speaking

still, a myopic dictate stammers
eight hours and *sleep hygiene* at the lectern

*

Centuries back the moon's disc high at cold daybreak
or at the summer dawn, all promise in the magpie's rattle
the slow shuttered opening of an eye
feet finding shoes on flagstones
bed pots of piss to cast by the nettles
water to draw again from the well

*

I sink back into second sleep again, rested —
the first light suggesting itself
at the curtain edge

3. Deprivation

What it might have been like// experiences// to access more
or were people trying to just shift their consciousness
sideways

You stay awake// the journey of the initiate
7 days and nights// just one of many practices

Most of the interesting stuff happened
around about 3 or 4 days onwards// from that moment on
that internal voice// that internal dialogue we all seem to have
was in rhyme// a whole day where everything was in rhyme

Things were communicated// a different form of communication
I was aphasic — after about 11 minutes or so
I got some noises out// some sylllables
my voice was much more resonant// syntax was different
I don't normally have access to

Latent functionality// balance of the hemispheres
how far you shift them// to inhibit the rational
doesn't comprehend it

Parameter glimpses// our reference points
our ancestors// perpetual rapture
understanding those words
phenomenally

4. Rest

Stillness — only
fridge hum and Wi-Fi, beyond
the black night under wet canopies

the rain has come like in the olden days
that smell, speaking me to the drinking
soil, the animals lap at fresh pools

again, the diesel rinsed off the plane
tree leaves, rivulets running into the
scale-shape of the bark

God let this city pause. God let it rest.
Away off I can hear it tugging and racing
God let its edges be porous, silence

leach in to the heart of it.
I will go to the river every sunset
and pray for that and every sunrise

cast in clay ears, offer mistletoe
vervain, oatstraw, float candles
in threes and sevens on its swell

Immigration enforcement

may you no   no
crawl the darkness
crawl the corner, park up
may you no   no

under this coral sky
then the light falling
turn the corner   stop
the van pulling in slow

under this dark sky
us building resistance
(know that)
gathering forces

all of our
intelligence

may you no   no
fat officer armoured, power-coward
crawl the dark streets   van
crawl the corner park up
and up to the door

a black feather
a black beak
a claw

disorientate
collapse

forget what you came for

Border

Young woman
white underarm handbag
slip-ons with high heels she was
just taller than the counter
where he was looking at her
and at her passport

He hands her a card
says *can you fill in these details*
can you read it, you're German yes
are you German
do you speak German

All ten of her fingers
pushing against the plastic counter
him holding the passport between
thumb and finger, then with both hands
he says *I don't think this is her*
to a second passport controller
who has come to stand behind his right shoulder

I glimpse the photo
the young woman next to me
the man at my counter asking
if I've just come from the Czech Republic
that there are two buses they are processing
no I say, *Germany*

We get back on the coach
the doors close
the coach pulls away

The driver stops to recount
folk at the front say that the young woman isn't there
pointing to the seat where she'd been sitting

Ja, he said
sie haben sie verhafftet

arrested, 14, 15, 16, 17...
her bags still on the seat
the bus drives off

An older women at the front tells us all
the bus doesn't wait if you're detained—
then reaches to the seat behind her
where the young woman had been sitting
and flicks through the magazines she'd been reading

Spell for Malic, aged 2
Calais, July 2016

Your smile will fill every continent —
we'll summon all the fire we can muster
to match the shine in you —   stand
you will take your long legs to the south
and to the north, open lungs, your mother
tongue and all the rest come singing
from your heart muscle

Your eyes will behold all the seas
as and when you choose, how they will watch
and know and inquire, and be defiant power
staying your laughter's breadth

Your mother's mother, and her mother
and her mother and hers, drive you on
into any headwind, no matter the dust
or razor wire, no matter the dark tunnel
or airless crossing stowed between cargo
pulse and soil, all their bones
witness your safe journey

You will be loved by multitudes
        they will come and come
everyday standing strong
wherever you tread —
feet kissing the ground
breathing all the winds in

Schooling

In docile pen
a learned management of the wild self
burying impulses, and lonely
only because everything
had been made all human —
tree family, bird family, stars
no elder took my hand to know

Odd sparks growing into sensation
momentary expansions of a self
some cameraderie
in the chase to the buzzer

I was sat at graph paper
coralled into small aspects
of contemporary push
bound into a corset
tied with thick, black lengths
of my mother's hair she cut short
when her babies came

We were taught the game
of emancipation (purchase and sell)
running the halls of our own interiors
often cold, always hungry

Savile Harris

how suddenly out from under the smother blanket
years of buried molestation
old men, here the truth seeping out like rancid milk

we always knew
something didn't ring well, this desire stifle
the flesh assassinator church, and the state of it

and now young bodies who have taken a lifetime
to name and give voice; the courage it took
to never say a word and now say something
unlocking, reliving it in the tissues, are speaking;

brave now you like the wind
opening the lie vaults, giving of your strength
unfolding cramped wings

that this whole show break trap
that in every momentary beat
we might begin to foster
some deep, communal repair

Raising them up

You are reinventing the wheel
never was a wheel anyway —
more hard surfaces
dim schooling
little beings taught the asphyxiate
of behaving behaviour

You are raising them up
clear thinkers   tuned
turning over leaf mould, knowing the stars
maths magic absorbed, word-play
crafted right at the gateway
no holds barred playing free jazz
with uncle so and so, immersed in silence
building fires with their best friend's mother
baking soda bread because it's quick
swimming the rivers, swimming the sea
sensing their limits
trusting their own judgement

They are writing left- and right-handed
in three languages —
hoards of other kids to race with
someone visits, teaches them
how to dance from centre
and see with their peripheral vision
and listen with their heart muscle
soft and strong, small ones
is how

Question

1. Spectrum

Fine sensitivity this
the room all muddle tongue, all afloat
going to cave in, swallowed like the sea bed
like white noise, like losing your balance
seventy voices talk and echo

Fine sensitivity this
word shape spill and hold you
an inhabitation, the labyrinth
the mind's ear talking —
sense as determined by whom
seeking a commons

The human spirit is in revolt, says
        I do not wish to speak
(now that it's all about speaking here)
but reside instead in a gossamer maze
multiplying fractions to decimal points
like litanies,
or sounding chords pitch perfect
soft moss and fur for comfort
        a version of shy
        where shy refuses
        where shy allows —

Fine sensitivity this the ubiquitous and complex
detailed drawings, graphite patterns, repetitions
consciousness amplified, agitated, othered

2. *Syndrome*

Born and raised
on a farm outside Vienna —
opal skies and sugar beet fields
Hans Asperger

the elder of two sons
had difficulty
finding friends

Syndrome describes
a collection of
symptoms & findings

Twisting his hands
in his pockets
solitary, ruminating
he was considered
a lonely, remote child

The word derives from
the Greek meaning
"concurrence"

It is said a love of language
sailed in him —
he quoted the poetry
of Franz Grillparzer
to uninterested classmates

Even in syndromes
with no known cause,
associated symptoms
lead researchers
to hypothesize

And then him quoting
himself, saying *he* said
and *Hans* thinks

that there exists
an unknown
underlying reason
for all the described
symptoms

And after school
him leant into haystacks
cowbells clanging and echoing
the herd lowing, their
high pungent sweetness
in the summer heat

3. Cowgirl

Temple Grandin in Western shirts and neckerchiefs
a grainy lens, a sifting of cattle dust
saying she noticed the animals got scared
when they had to walk straight lines to slaughter —
"so now we got curved chutes"

4. Cowboys

"... each individual is different
some have amazing ability
to retain information
think at a level of detail and depth
or excel in math or code.

It's a talent pool
that we want to continue
to bring to Microsoft!"

5. Noise

Sugar cubes/ arm scar/ staggered vaccines
— *never the same since*
Mercury in seafood. Colistin in pig fat
the wheat crop dowsed in Glyphosate
Malathion in two out of every three loaves
trace neuroleptics in the water —

Ultrasound, ultrasound and microwave
and twenty eight wifi servers in one block
and the contract small print
that advises
hold your
mobile phone
one inch
away
from
your
head

6. Quiet

I keep trying to take you aside
there's something I've been wanting to talk about
I have a Question for you

Casting back

Young self, waiting
in the waiting room —
I lean back through the years
to my body's paused edge;
a urine sample
a test stick turning blue

And let me tell you

I could have run drunk
   charge   spark
the spiralling life that had entered in
positive she said, it's positive

There I was. Can you see me?
Chewing at raw carrots, ginger
on the beach, quell the nausea
I sat and sat by the water
each swell and suspension
falling onto the shingle
then pulling out
sucking through the stones

Big ocean   and in me
        this liminal ground
bearing life, a co-creation

I was naming my agency
in the vast unfolding
like my great, great grandmothers
always had, a hidden history
I was grasping back

Let me tell you

I was hoop jumping, doctors signing
approval papers. Small room —
his smirk, syringe, stethoscope

a calendar for counting

Then I was sat on warm park grass
the beginning of this goodbye
a drug dissolving into my tissues
   into my soul story
like black cohosh might
like pennyroyal might
   parsley sage, rosemary and thyme
      for she once was
like rue, like tansy

Two days later, plastic mattress
crunching under my weight
pessary against the mouth of my womb
the pains pulled in. It was a few of us
that day on the ward, avoiding eye contact
making steady relay to the bathroom
blood coming, cramps
and cardboard bedpans to catch

Let me speak of this

At the end of those hours, quiet, alone
last passing all out of me, small thing came
the curled arc of body, head, hands, feet
a miniature umbilical cord
small rubbery white

I could have laid it in the centre
of the palm of my hand
tiny, amphibian

I sat in the toilet
and drew every silent breath
in and out, in long, slow seconds
and I looked and I looked
this incredible thing —
inhabiting the paradox
death and birth in the same breath
a rite
   of passage

Afterwards, home again, free from watch
I stepped out to the wind and grasses
and sounds heaved up guttural from in me
like I'd never heard before
and never heard again since

I marked the come and return
planted willow sticks by the river
plunged under three times, and later
wresting back from hospital file and lab
we made a closing together, a ceremony
small thing I shaped and laid in earth
a bundle of smoking sticks burning an ashen drift

I speak of this

In me a residing power

I speak of this

Life wilder and bloodier than the
cleric and the lawmen fodder
robed and white-coated
denying the matrix we gateway
pushing us *across the foam*
and State to State —
the body as battleground

We cast back the authority
they claim — striking en masse
making Black Friday to the Bishops
wearing green pañuelos
repealing, reinstating
remembering

I say this

You, you keep your ghoulish
colour fetus photos —
fetish placards you hold up
as grotesque moral armour

blocking pavements
in sickly, silent vigil

You, with your precious life
and rallying for life and marching
for life, robbing language of meaning
and obsessing over viability; a fetal heartbeat
and your heartbeat machines —
a machination of control
rolling back Roe v. Wade.

It is *ours*
this spirit/matter — in us
our bodies
within
the greater body
of
the holy spirit
— in us

    this liminal ground

It is ours
choosing
where and how
    and if
    and when

Chitty

I recall
her small frame
resilience.

Long ninety years of life
a bit of soup, some yoghurt
soft for the old gums
and her yelling
and her resistance
and her terror.

How she was handled
lifted, washed, wiped
minimum wage haste
Watch her, they said
watch her, she bites.

I recall
the smell
roast beef and overcooked veg
piled into the blender. A grey mush
the medication crushed in, spike
served up. A napkin wedged hard
down the front of her dress at the neck.

Tired, overstretched women
their own laundry left, children to care for
between shifts, dead to themselves, shouting
dinner time, dinner time at her.

Beautiful old woman
I don't forget
who bit the hand that fed her
and touched her how she didn't
fucking want to be.

Good sport

August 2011

The streets are quiet
4pm boarded up
Sainsbury's shutting early
windows panned in
the Argos, the bank, the bookies

In Peckham they have come in made a Peace Wall
post-it notes for positive messages, all

I heart Peckham
No more riots
though in amongst them
We should make it a weekly event

On East Street market
everybody is talking about it
no post-it notes but one guy
just ahead of me saying

The problem is
the police are like a disease

August 2012

She was working at the Olympics
feeding the athletes

said her foot is sometimes
like it's burning now
and her knee is in pain

sometimes she said we were stood in the fridge
like one big fridge the size of this flat
three, four hours
then straight out in front of the hotplates again

and nowhere to ever sit down
and they only gave us half an hour for lunch

and sometimes when we got to the canteen
which was a ten minute walk away
there wasn't anything left for us to eat

Bath

Warm
the days still open
autumn late come abundant
plum ripe, yew berries red
rosehips the hillside down.

Here
place made museum
a steward rushed over
the second I had stooped
said I shouldn't touch the water.

People wired to audio tours
paid their money, attraction
camera snap
dull the senses.

Beneath the pump room restaurant
passaged recesses and cased artefacts
video projections on the ancient wall
all walkway arrows and the gift shop
you slam into
right next to the running water.

Underneath the pillar remains
the steps in archways
under statues and deities
and faded mosaic, I visited
the strong warm spring.

Source emerging magic
of vapour and heat
(she rushed over
said I shouldn't touch the water)
where I bathed my hands.

In these last days my friend

At the base of you, your own
leaves a yellow carpet in the green
park, each breeze layering them gently
under your thin centre

You have always been bold
I have often admired you
you're ahead of all the others
who will soon follow

The shock of lemon and yolk
making radiance to rot back
root food that will turn to the sky
in you again come spring

Burst before the fall —
bright before the bare winter

Lochend

Storm
a rare wind that pulls at the willows
pushes at them, suck
opening the windows
making the houses lonesome

The buildings
The wind

It was coal fires, back greens
the local park, the local shops
1930's clad grey, people shipped
out and then shipped in to

The wind
The buildings

Old man on the street telling me
his mother *raised all five children*
in that house, didn't want to own it
                we'd have bought it for her
said she hoped somebody else
could raise a family in it
when she'd gone

My neighbour running in and out, slam
on his mobile, middle of the night
dropping his needles in the stairwell

The stair cleaners mopping bleach
never hear a peep out of 'naked Willie'
upstairs, sitting in front of UV rays

The women opposite
nesting their private property
                we're going travelling
                we're going to rent it out

put a security door on the close
in preparation
was only on a week before kids
put a brick through the glass

Quickening

Flit of charcoal powder
switching on the wing
then gone, only a trace left
a thin vibration amongst the overcast

You know they're still there
you search for them flocking at bladed angle
then they thicken split second — fine dust
to dark coal seams in the air currents again

Bold fragile they ribbon figures of eight
twisting swathes in unison
over the waves at sundown
heading west across the tide

It's cold here
the cold that cuts through to the skin
the starlings make the long dusk dance
breakers suck in and back
the wind lacing through our lungs
permeable sacs

Their flight is summons
it carries us out there —
up and wheeling and dropping
quickening us out over the deep water

Trilogy for my Dad's Passing
— 1. Visiting with my Dad

Paid people to nurse my father, no hearth —
there at the last of him, getting to small pieces of intimacy
sliding our hands together, his old bruised elbow in my palm
between spoonfuls and tired lungs frail back into the pillow.

Close together, a few words, the ward noise receded
then as we leant out it swelled back in again —
ECG bleep, trolleys wheeling sticky on the flooring.

Old fella, tissue paper skin
pulse ticking like thin wire
under my fingers.

…

Home again, curled on his side in the warm
semi-dark of the back room —
the fragile hush like a newborn in the house
tread softly someone is sleeping, someone is leaving us
and down to so little, his pyjamas falling
from his frame, that one time when he got dressed
as if to go out
his trousers ballooning around him
on new red braces.

…

It landed in me, looking back, all those days
trying to listen in the glare —
everybody shouting at the aged like infants
at the elderly like idiots, trampling around
like lunatics shouting *are you OK?* at the dying.

And that one night, not able to speak
knocking at his chest bone with his knuckles
Does it hurt dad, is it racing?

The watching and waiting
being with and tending to
There's still a chance, he said and how I couldn't hold
the tears, never did cry with him like that before.

I sat, he lay back, slept, grew more tired —
the visiting hours stretched into the winter darkness
the leaves fell, it got colder.

Snow scene

It’s mild and raining
Christmas is start up again
metal fencing surround
small sombre trees.

All around the wired island
festivity turn, trot
fill up every last cupboard
pawn the space at the back of the skull.

On the main drag a huge plastic bubble
filled with fake, air-blown snow invites you in
£10 for a photograph.

Money is running and running
cosmetics, cookware, cameras, phones
paper bags dissolving in the wet.

The frame for this —
all the stars strung bright
constellating
in the power
(not this
undone accumulation of poverty)
where all the riches are.

New Year's Eve

The sky blasts open red
then cracks green —
the crows emerge as if from the wood
a sudden exodus born from the black
they pour out crash into the branches
wing clap race
circling through the tops
beating round in eery silence

Only the sound of their clattering
colliding panic, they return
to perch a second, then are gone
in flight again from rest

I whisper soothing words
to their distress
into the darkness

The fire colour stutters and bangs
once or twice more, then it's over
The crows slowly settle back

Trilogy for my Dad's Passing
— 2. Rites

Cremation.
Collecting the ashes.
Scattering the ashes.
The Thames, Winter.

We made it at the alloted hour, a patient observance
navigated our familiar tensions that were circling and cawing
clipping the breath between the shoulder blades.

There was bright frost on the ground, floral tributes all
out of seasonal kilter, the filters on the crematorium
keeping the air fume-clear from the furnaces.

Ahead of us mourners arrived for the slot before ours
swelling in black at the entrance porch
went in a while, emerged, and left.

And then it came, your willow casket weighting us
into presence, the grief open again as we carried you
small candles, peace we placed all around
you and just us and the chapel calm.

Journey fire. Farewell.
How the wilds opened out that night I lost myself to.
It was dark and radiant the orbit I was wheeling in.

…

And then the box of your ground bone
small white coral pieces and white dust

The inferno that took your body
melted and blazed, the final
charging of the day, Kali grinning in

You weigh a tonne I said to you
carrying you between the river bridges.

. . .

The south, south westerly wind
mute, overcast, New Year's Day
for the last of you to the low tide
four carnation sprays   sundown

Then the urn's paper liner to flame
a brief, bright orange flare
at the river's edge.

And later it rained.
And the sea came for you in the night.

The January Man

Oh the January man he walks abroad
in woolen coat and boots of leather
— Trad. English folk song

Everybody stepping about in cold January
Someone fired a gun at the starting line
the arena is empty, three people turned up
went home again. Freezing fog

*

Dormouse
your heart slowed, 6-13 beats per minute
the frozen leaf mould insulate
fur, fat, in hungering slumber

The sun is still casting low into the retina
the night is still stretching into dark arms

*

Underground
Rush hour
The iron supplement advert
Are you tired of feeling tired?

*

The geese in arrowed formation
calling us to attention in the still winter
their syncopated pulse, honking
on the downward wing

You stop and watch
It is the watching that counts

Trilogy for my Dad's Passing
— 3. Visiting with my Dad

The recollection like dream retrieval
like grasping at air   a kind of panic
in the back of me behind my heart somewhere
the finality — your gentle hands, beautiful fingers
thumbs that bent like mine do.

The water, the water you're in now, shifting sands
strong currents and easy flow round the piers
boat moorings, sometimes river, sometimes salt sea
the flux of your final resting place
traveller.

The brackish portal, cradles and rocks your being
into me at the bank, the devotional wide
of gone and everywhere
and nowhere in everything.

I pull away, leave the river to wash and sigh
and rise and empty out again.

New Clear

1.
Hiroshima Nagasaki
                    if we all wear velvet gloves
can we put you back   black box
lower you down   chant
          arrowtip never to target —
no target to find   mankind
marching on gravel, hands up in the air
fade out/the sound of crystal clear
running water.

It's too late

Wait — someone said something
about an icewall: 1.4 kilometers of coolant
to freeze the groundwater around the spill
leaching from a thousand hastily constructed
tanks, 355,000 tons of radioactive water
400 more washing out every day —

A lead cover falls, a candle blows out
it's cold, it's frantic, there were news
flashes, then no more
news flashes
then it was quiet —

just the constant, slow leak of cesium hotspots
for all the steel walls they have raised
in the sea bed round the crippled plant
collapsed at the edge of the ocean clutching at its sides
the hot, hot water pouring through its fingers.

2.
On the ocean floor, fissures where tectonic plates
are slowly yawning apart or around volcanic activity
— hydrothermal vents — extreme heat —
the water far past boiling, fathoms down molton ore seeps
making black smoker chimneys in the pitch darkness

the midnight zone.
Such force, as quake, from here
that pushed a tsunami to the shore.

3.

Silence. Doors fallen from frames. Dry brush weed in cracks. A small breeze through abandoned buildings. One woman still goes back in to feed the cats. Derelict road blocks. Shop shelves hanging empty. Children's toys tipped on their sides. Rusting bikes, rusting cars. The Geiger counter clicking high in the grasses.

One sievert dose — *radiation sickness, nausea*
Five sieverts — *kill you within a month*
Ten sieverts — *dead in weeks*
The seventy three sievert tolerant robots they sent in to Fukishima,
just faltering malfunction
Hot concrete, hot metal, hot air — recent reactor levels there
reading five hundred and thirty sieverts per hour.

4.

Look away, look away. History cowers guilt. Who? Gap
When? Shows us tight jawlines, jaws clenching —
                    Now no one saying anything
                    Anything at all.

My mother tells me my Uncle had said —
          Er blieb dann manchmal die Nacht.
          He used to pass through. In the '70s.
          Nuclear scientist. They invited him.
          On the way out to Japan.
          Das hatte er damals schon gesagt —
— that they shouldn't build it there
on a faultline —

5.

                    back   *black box*
lower you down   *chant*
                    mankind

hands up
fade out/the sound of crystal clear
running water

back black box
lower you down chant
mankind
hands up
fade out/the sound of crystal clear
running water

back black box
lower you down chant
mankind
hands up
fade out/the sound of crystal clear
running water

back black box
lower you down chant
mankind
hands up
fade out/the sound of crystal clear
running water

Prayer for the Blackfish

Roam all your seven tonnes
hundreds of miles
No cracking your teeth
trying to chew your way out of tanks
            clap, clap making you formation jump
young calf wailing for its mother in isolated pool
No dorsal fin collapse —
            the mournful psychosis of captivity

You sound the waters
            pulsed calls, low frequency pops
high directional whistles   and clicks, speaking
in distinct dialects from phonic lips
pod by pod, your intimate proximity

your song which travels
four and a half times faster through ocean
than air, those long waves in the waves —
                        millisecond clicks in trains,
projected through rounded forehead blubber
an acoustic lens sending beams
to bounce
and echo back
into the listening fat of your jaw bones:
all the shapes, their composition and speed
                        at swim to hear

No shipping traffic
or military radar
disorientate you, beached
your lovers coming to you there
            small buckets, wet towels
watching your blowholes blow
shading you from the hot sun
close to your huge eyes
telling you
            you can do it
            the tide is turning

it’s not long now
it’s not so long

No trash vortex
plastic islands
oceanographers reading cargo spills:
a measure of currents in a swell of
Nike sneakers
small rubber ducks
bits of lego
suspended
in the Atlantic

No more this toxic love story
shrink-wrapped and sealant, sweating
osmotic micro beading
into marine cell walls
from exfoliator, toothpaste, plastic silt
in shampoo bottle, flip-flops, nylon cord
oil drum canisters, polyester microfibres
making filaments in Blackfish breath
lungs, them ingesting thin skeins

Lulu, they named her
all washed up dead on Tiree
one of a pod of eight, snagged in polypropelene rope

her skeleton in the National Museum now. What use?
Pcb levels in her blubber, a hundred times higher
than would have consequences —
never calved
and there’ll be no more calves now
and not long it’s said before
all the Blackfish
will be gone from these waters

Whoever we pray to, however we pray
let us pray harder

Sing hymns to the oceans
let us do this together

Renewal — Pool

One strong lungful
then diving deep
for the oxygen
exchange

Cool blue
and that muffled
silence under
the sound above

There, the long slow
breathing today out
and yesterday out
and that time
ten years ago out

Renewal — River

I slip in naked
kiss the current, glide towards
the alder root buckle

the river is bottomless

In the channel, tipped back floating
the sun burning high-midsummer
clouds like the white of an eye
I pull myself through the tow
in slow strokes

Those warm, cool then cold pockets
to melt into, be charged by
with the trout and minnows
not so long til it will be all ice
the fish dormant at the river bed
barely breathing

The shock of blue damselflies
my breasts up to the air, my long body
trailing below the translucent, olive surface

Every year this baptismal font
that bears me back into life again
drift, dive, wend
everything slowed
to the water's pace

I land at the bank feet sinking into the thick
clay base, toes sucking the mud between them
stoop to lever myself up, rising out, sharp
this moment   exhilaration   earth
the water running off
through the hair
between my legs

Renewal — Sea

I speak to this moment, all sticky with salt
peeling the sea lettuce off my thighs, my feet

crystalised sand, the tide drawing in and out
like the sound of my blood, and the memory

of my mothers, and my grandmothers
that amniotic amplification, generation

after each, swimming and surfacing. I sit
and reconcile the beauty I find myself in

and all possibility, with the torn and lacking
and all that violates and binds

Say *Salt sea, wide sea, open waters*
open waters, salt sea, wide sea
wide water, salt sea, open
open waters, wide water, salt

Renewal — Tides

Poverty —

Like the novitiate
entering the enclosure
lying prostrate
on stone floor
breathing surrender
in and out

I float in the cold

Chastity —

I am swimming under the waves
gazing entranced through tides
bright widemouthed fish
and coral waving
in the liquid glass

I am naked, I am turning

Obedience —

It is silent
I look up
just below the surface, sunlight shining
translucent through red-green weeds
I am no longer in the speaking
I do not want to speak

In the push, in the pull

Untitled

As before there is nothing to say
just the silent wide and widening

someone tells me
that the atom is empty

just as the tiny wren fills
the woods with song

Maslow's Hierarchy

Mr
Maslow,
I'm just not
sure but they still
wheel you out Left,
Right and Centre buying
into the same white-man-looking
white-man-speaking truths for everyone's
needs: banded, an ordered layering divorced.
Mr Maslow, they still reference you. Yes to a baseline;
food and fire, but you have split the ancestors from the
hearth and offerings, you have placed song and story 4 tiers
up that might be precisely *how* someone builds their home, and
knows it nesting in the soil between not just trees, but trees known
by name and requested for the fruits they bear and given thanks to. I see
evolution, that image fed my childhood, white-man-walking-upright on two legs
into office, courtroom, battle, all aspiration and ambition, achieving and accomplishment
dry throat, feet in tight shoes, reaching some disintegrated mountain top of the Self. I trust
you meant well Mr Maslow, thank you for your pyramid, to some extent I enjoy the colours.

Make no bones about it

Hollow flight stems, the flotsam
hooked in the wrack and grasses
all drying in the salt wind —
gannet's keel, sheep's vertebrae
jaw of a mountain hair

Listen

Brittle, bring it close, we lie with it within
bending, deep in the marrow, sponge
hydrating, renewing, reshaping itself
over and over as we tread, curve, carry
feel it in your bones

Listen

Swing
dance them
settle in

Listen

The long thin Japanese chopsticks
that pick and pass the remains
patella, pelvis, scapula, sternum —
placing them upright in the urn
dispelling the myth of '*ashes*':
here, the cremulator that grinds
the dead to powder

Listen

The top rib that dances on the breath
the bottom that fans the bellows —
and below, the heavy plumb line
a wide anchoring keystone

Listen

Hammer, anvil, stirrup, cochlea —
the small, snail spiral of the inner ear
hear the call of the rag and boneman

Listen

Femur stacks in Cambodian killing fields
Skulls of the disappeared in Chilean desert

Listen

Arnhem Land bones in Canberra warehouse
Lakota bones in Colorado Museum

Listen

Listen

Listen

Manna-hata

What would it be
if there was no traffic in Manhattan

only people moving
the sound of steps and voices

and what would these enormous
buildings be good for now

if money was of no matter
and the land handed back

Some white folks from Alabama on the Amtrak

It's our 40th

we're taking trains all over for three weeks

Our son, decided

he wanted to be a police officer

He said

Daddy, I want a badge, a gun and a car

In actual fact

they said

he said

I want a gun, a car and a badge

in that order

They said

We said

Honey —

You make sure you protect yourself first

we'll take care of anything we need to after

Öngtupqa
The Grand Canyon

As you step to the edge
of the southern rim
the canyon comes up
and drops away
stretching into
its hundreds of miles

Like crescendo and take-off
'hallelujah' and 'amen' —
the hot, red rock and green,
home of the Hopi salt trails in
and somewhere far, far down
the cool Colorado river

Faultline

The sidewalk urine is caramelised
we are in the country of the last things
shopping carts, black bags stuffed with cans
the streets unhinged, roaming dehydrated
or lolling in car seats on the corner

Stringy calves kick at trash on Valencia, someone
fills water at the dog park fountain on 7th, a glassy-eyed
woman falls on her cases, laughing in a heap on Broadway
young woman, barefoot, eyes in absent, band of red spray paint
across her knees is twisted on a mesh metal bench at Pier 39

I think the security guy on 18th is telling me
She's Annette
but he's saying *She's a nut*

There is a woman crumpled in the piss on 24th
three officers, blue latex gloves, frame her distress

Men stoop and loiter
and yell
and deal pills on Mission
and talk politics
and wheel denim trousers tied off with string
            where the knees used to be
and stagger liquor paths into the traffic

Easy Rider is rifling in the bins, thick white spittle
on his chin, everywhere old bones sifting through waste
asking for spare change or holding cardboard signs
Hungry as hell at the stop lights

There is some kind of Exodus
but no one is leaving

Ahwahnee
Yosemite

The sun is setting
on the cedar chapels
and across the high Sierras

Ahwahnechee
your glacier cathedral
your temple remains everywhere

My father came to me on the journey in
the way rainbows colour the falls here
you might almost miss

I leave entirely altered
giving thanks
crow stone river

All the white rock turning pink
then plunging into cold grey
and the valley floor gloaming

Foot clinic, Catholic Worker, Skid Row, LA

Arkansas...
Got a son, 30 years old...
yeh, I call him every now and then

One winter was so wet I got alley feet
s'more painful than a toochache Robert tells me

Yeh, I'm waiting for them to get me a house
but I'm having some problems with my ID

The streets house tents, blocks and blocks of them —
the foot clinic, like a weekly prayer meeting in the courtyard
round buckets of soapy water and foot files is where I'm washing tools
sweeping skin shavings and sitting talking until the morning is done

Big Jo is shouting and singing
fainted at the foot clinic last week
and is only just back out of hospital

Silent Michael, mid 50's, soft eyes, knuckle tattoos
getting all of his thick toenails filed down
or lifted away, corns and calouses bandaged

Everybody leaving with a clean pair of socks

I can see the ancestors —
they are walking in broken shoes
with blue hair and no teeth, with bags and carts

They are calling *Happy feet day* through the fencing

Herman Wallace

While I was dreaming myself into this body
crawling spittle, cutting teeth, nursery school
and school milk, hot sun on plastic paddling pool
sports days, sweating tests, leaving home

While I was asking, refusing, finding
by flames rounding driftwood
on shores foaming shingle spits
or in friends' houses, or my own
or any places I chose by train, on foot
cycling into headwind
or with the wind at my back

All of those years

For all of the years of the whole of my life
you, locked in a 6 x 9 foot cell

> *The majority of my life has been in a cage*
> *The majority of my life —*
> *I came in this cell at 31 years old man*
> *I'm 69 now*

The solitary hours
hung out of sunlight
stark depravity
your dignity blazing

> *I'm good. Just get me out of here.*

I turned the pages of the paper
and read of your death
just three days
after your release

I peel back thick pomegranate skin
the red juice runs down my wrists
lay the seeds and pith on the ground for you

The skies they open, they open
The skies they open, they open
they open

Troy Davis

1. Defence

And so tell me. I put it to you.
Something about a car lot. Burger King.
A drive by shooting. A white

T-shirt. A .38 caliber pistol. And bullet casings.
Seven witnesses said they saw him do it.
Two witnesses said he confessed he'd done it.

Seven witnesses recanting their testimonies;
saying *police pressure to co-operate*
or didn't know what they were signing.

The court describing the defence
as *largely smoke and mirrors*.
The defence naming this *cruel*

and unusual punishment — twenty years
several stays of execution, once, just less
than two hours before he was to die.

2. Photograph: *1932*

On the left hand side, young men are smiling, the large crowd of white people is gathered beneath the tree in the darkness. Apparently in many photos there is a pointer, someone who is pointing to the hanging bodies, like a warning, a threat. Bottom right, a young girl with blond hair, about 8 years old is grinning, a wide grin, direct to camera. There is activity in the photograph, excitement. The atmosphere was described as being like a picnic, a holiday. Someone took the picture, a souvenir, later they were made into postcard collections that were sent to loved ones in the mail

...a great day we had...

3. Prosecution

…convict leasing// in the aftermath of slavery// when one sees the transformation of some of the huge slave plantations into places where prisoners work// slavery and the mass incarceration// the history of slavery// the failure to entirely abolish the consequences of slavery// haunted by the institutions connected with slavery…

4. Reform: *France 1789*

The sharp blade
bettering the blunt axe
the breaking wheel.

Long after *The Maiden*
had been cutting heads off
in Scotland, French physician
Monsieur Guillotin
was tempering the barbaric
on   the way   to
its Abolition.

He didn't put his name to it —
that was the whole point.

5. The Last Poets: *November 2016*

Remembering him
on stage saying, he thought
Black Lives Matter
was a *weak* demand —

that black lives have *always* mattered —
what he was interested in
was Black *Power*.

6. Reform: *Oklahoma1977*

OPENING SHOT: ARCHIVE FOOTAGE

Voiceover:
The Reverend Bill Wiseman —
A young Oklahoma pastor and legislator...
... he loved the game of politics...

EXTERIOR LONG SHOT, MORNING

Voiceover:
... now retracing his theological steps...

INTERIOR, CHURCH, CLOSE UP, INTERVIEW

Bill Wiseman (BW):
... the motivation to get re-elected, have everybody like you,
everybody, lots of times worked at cross purposes
with what that still, small voice would say...

Interviewer:
So what did you do?

BW:
I made the wrong mistake —
I just felt sick, I was actually executing people
I knew it was wrong and I should have voted
against it but I didn't...

Voiceover:
... pen pushing, on the tracks of his guilt, to expiate his shame...

BW:
So I jotted it down on a yellow legal pad:
"An intravenous saline drip shall be started
in the prisoner's arm, into which shall be introduced
a lethal injection consisting of an ultra-short-acting barbiturate
in combination with a chemical paralytic."

Voiceover:
... making the first jurisdiction in the world
to adopt lethal injection...

BW:
... making it easier for judges and juries... in a sense
I bear the responsibility for those deaths, I'm sorry for what I did
I'm aware of my responsibility, it keeps me tied to the problem.
And the problem is we're killing people.

INTERIOR, NONDENOMINATIONAL CHAPEL,
UNIVERSITY OF CENTRAL OKLAHOMA, EARLY MORNING

BW in the pulpit reading from Psalm 102:
For the Lord looked down from his holy place on high;
from the heavens he beheld earth;
that he might hear the groan of the captive
and set free the condemned to die

FADE OUT

7. The Last Supper

Sweet potato fries.
Burger. Chicken wings.
Steak. Soda & lime.

Alcohol is prohibited.
Requests for cigarettes and bubble gum
have been turned down.

A significant number of inmates forgo
the 'special meal', defiance/ lack of appetite/
spiritual reasons. Inmates tired of co-operating
with these rituals of death.

Troy Davis declined — said
This meal will not be my last.

8. Reform: *March 2017*

Reporter: We turn now to   yes, I can hear you, can you hear us? OK, go ahead —

Campaigner: Pentobarbital used to euthanise animals   yes, people administering the execution drugs called *medical staff* the *killing time* used to be midnight   changed a few years ago to make it easier on staff and witnesses,   yes, we are working so medical products don't get used in this way   a growing chorus of   European pharma companies   research that suddenly they were sourcing *untested* drugs   through *un-conventional* means   a division of Johnson & Johnson said   no their paralytic would *not* be used in that way   And Oklahoma *especially* enthusiastic with the needle   And Arkansas rushing 8 executions through because a lethal injection drug was about to go past its expiration date.

Reporter: Thank you. Thank you for talking to us.

9. Last Words: *September 21, 2011, Georgia Diagnostic and Classification Prison*

Well, first of all I'd like to address the MacPhail family.
I'd like to let you all know that despite the situation
I know all of you still are convinced that I'm the person
that killed your father, your son and your brother,
but I am innocent.
The incidents that happened that night was not my fault.
I did not have a gun that night.
I did not shoot your family member.
But I am so sorry for your loss. I really am -- sincerely.
All that I can ask is that each of you look deeper into this case
so that you really will finally see the truth.

I ask to my family and friends that you all continue to pray,
that you all continue to forgive. Continue to fight this fight.

For those about to take my life,
may God have mercy on all of your souls.

God bless you all.

Justice for A

For The London Campaign against Police and State Violence

All three policemen
same scrunched tension round their mouths
crumpling their lips against their teeth as they testify
                                        yes ma'am that's correct ma'am

The stiff formality *my learned friend* of order & power
everyone knows their place & flexes themselves
within those bounds feeling the edges

All rise (reluctant) she *will* command that
dragging her heels to the exit til
every   one   was   standing

Five minute recesses
or my back will seize up she said
& breaking for lunch
we'll reconvene to sit again at 2

Black woman
White cops
White court

Foregone, a guilty verdict —
Stephen Lawrence ghosting the bench

For the family and friends who fought 27 years for justice
Tuesday 26th April 2016

After the Hillsborough final inquest verdict

Granular VHS, red and white
strip, pitch, the typical
stadium throb, six minutes in
they call off the game
the camera scanning, young
folks dragging themselves
over the fencing lying on the
ground breathless, the
surging crush lifting people
onto the balcony like
ragdolls, it was four deep dead
at the front.

And the view was clear from
the surveillance terrace
but the call was for police
dogs not medical support
and at 3.15pm while people
were dying, Chief
Superintendant David Ducken-
field lied about the
exit gate he had had opened to
let people in.

The police that beat folk back
as they tried to climb
and the ambulances that came
but were just parked up
outside and the cops told to
line up across the stadium
guided only by a terror of los-
ing control of the crowd.

The young men hauling adver-
tising hoardings as
stretchers They're dying in
there, they're all dying in there
and the father on the turf with
the bodies of both his
daughters on the ground by his
side saying Help me,
please God, not both of them,
they're all we've got.

The dead on the dirty, make-
shift morgue floor. The
police coroner ordering blood
alcohol level checks on
all who died and the police
photographer sent out to
'gather evidence' taking pic-
tures of the litter at the
turnstiles.

That rapid manufacture of
narrative; drunken hooligan,
the working class mob, while
ruthless, institutional
self-defence buried its negli-
gence and prejudice under
piles of systematic deceit; hun-
dreds of police officer
statements edited of criticism
or comment before
they went to the inquiry.

That one black and white pho-
tograph, people's faces
rammed against the wire
mesh, the aftermath, bent
metal railings, clothing strewn
across the gaping empty,
the bereft, the broken. Those
ninety six faces on the
memorial wall you run the
cursor over, one short
paragraph about each life and
the cause and the
approximate time of death.

That unanimous final vote.
Unlawful killing. Inside the
courtroom applause, hugging,
tears. And afterwards
friends and family stood to-
gether one more time
and sang.

Uncle Phil

Witness statement

Name: ———
Case number: ———
Age: ————
Occupation: ————

I —— of —— am the Claimant in this claim. The facts in this statement come from my personal experience.

1. *... for ages I was anonymous// didn't want to speak about it// shut down// like this self-imposed gagging order// everyone else was speaking// speaking on my behalf // not wanting to be recognised but wanting to be heard//*

2. *... promised the world to everybody// a lot of his training// always tell you what he thought you wanted to hear// some people are just like that// never know how much of that was his training// his nature// so much to unpick there// never going to unpick it really// a lot of mirroring// a tactic they used// bought drum and bass records// get into things I was into// shared interests// guitar lessons// joined a band// things to ingratiate him// seem popular// probably things he wanted to do// living a fantasy life// part of the trade craft// mixing that// more convincing// if it's a bit real//*

3. *... really enjoyed the life he was leading as Mark Stone// also enjoyed the job he was doing as Mark Kennedy// training methods// building a legend// using bits of truth// bits of your real life// his brother was the only person from his real life that came into his undercover persona// a lot of the time he was going to visit his brother// some of the time when he was going home to his family// using that as a reason why he was out of the country// they always insisted on using married officers// 'something to come back to'// atrocious// the wife another woman who they don't give a shit about, and kids// I was going to meet his brother// last chunk of time I was with him he wasn't with the police anymore// holes started to appear in his story// going off piste// not being supported// police would never have allowed*

him to introduce someone from his real life to somebody in his undercover life//

4. *... every single one of them that we know had long-term relationships used breakdown as a reason to be leaving// cruel way to leave// worrying about your safety// searching for you// the reason they use it is because it's very very fucking convincing// they are losing their minds// he was disappearing, going away for longer// when he came back he was weird, he wasn't himself// coming apart as a person// one of the longest ones in// 7 years// 5 was the limit// there was the G8 in Germany coming up// had good connections for that// could well have been the reason he was left in//*

5. *... found his passport// confronted him// name and identity// some shady past, all seemed so believable// in the drugs trade with somebody who'd been shot// responsibility to his family// bringing those kids up as if they were his own// if I'd stepped back and just listened to the words it would have been obvious to me it was bullshit// just the emotion// I still believe the emotion, the emotion was real// he cried so much, we held each other and cried all night// only when he went away and I was on my own and I got to reflect on some of the things he'd said// subsequent things happened// not really backing it up//*

6. *... yeh, it's funny, I was really protective of// that I had met up with him// to give him a piece of my mind// didn't want anybody knowing// everybody went a bit insane around that time// people accusing other people of colluding with him// felt quite hounded by anonymous voices on the internet// really judged// some of the things people think we should or shouldn't have done// telling me that my responses had been wrong// how the fuck dare they tell me what it was like// part of my insanity at that time was that I had to read everything that everybody wrote// after an article you'd get 50 peoples comments// from Mark himself, occasionally, or 'I used to work for the cops'// so little information or real facts about what was going on// trying to look for clues everywhere// trying to look for answers on the internet, I was trying to look for him — even though not really him — but the him I thought I knew// still trying to find I think, on the internet//*

7. *... I'd be like, I'm going mad, why am I looking for him everywhere// did for years// every time I would travel anywhere// on a motorway or at services I was always thinking I'm going to bump into him// realised I had been walking around carrying what I was going to say to him// wasn't even aware that I was carrying it// was walking round in a bit of a daze at that time// one big long flashback// be cycling round and my brain would just be completely in the past and everything that had happened and then I'd get where I was going and almost not really remember the cycle// in that kind of a state a lot of the time// often staying with — and she came back and said// she'd bumped into him// and I said now I'm going to be doubly thinking that I'm going to bump into him everywhere and I can't live like that// rang him there and then// phone number still worked which was a bit of a shock// exposed him in October// this was February// said I've got to meet up with you// don't want to sit with what I am going to say to you playing round my head// think it is totally reasonable, at the time I was like, people are going to hate me for this but now I'm like, who the fuck would hate me// yeh, totally// there was a huge amount of that// things people were writing on the internet// I suggested to meet// nearest pub to a random train station// he said he was going to come on his own, I said I was going to bring someone but they were going to sit somewhere different// only when I got into the pub that I realised it was Valentines day, and there was couples on all the tables having candlelit dinners ...//*

8. *... I did ask him things// all the awkward questions// how could he say he loved me and still do that, how could it really be love if it's based on so much lies// lots of things that I needed to ask// all the hard things that I'd wanted to say to him// how it was for me// what he had put me through// became obvious very quickly that he didn't have answers// didn't know because he had no idea why he did a lot of the things, or was really feeling, or what was real and what was not// even if he did, I can't believe a word he says ever again so there's no point asking// half way through that I realised I wasn't ever going to get what I wanted// never going to be an explanation// I mean it was odd because he looked like him and smelt like him and all of that// had been so current and so raw that we were in a relationship and in love at the time// felt like one of those really*

ridiculous film scripts// if it was a film we probably would have got together against all the odds and blah, you know// I mean that's what I'd said to him, that this isn't a film, and you're not the hero and you're not going to get the girl// was as if part of him thought he would make it alright somehow// he'd sent me an email saying// you could forgive me// I'll introduce you to my mum after all// I'm sure we can work through it// basically sent him one about why that was never going to happen//amazed that he thought it possibly even ever could//

9. *... want to believe I can recognise love when I see it, everybody wants to think that// still think I do, but// there was so much lies// think that in there I did see a good person// I'm sure I did, but then I'm sure there is in everyone// for other people the story was more black and white, you know there's our side there's their side it was really clear// for me it made me realise the complexity of people// nobody's pure evil and nobody is purely good either, everybody's a real complex mix// how to sit with all of that, you know, for me, for my future relationships, my sense of self, knowing how much of that was real and how much of that was bullshit// never going to actually really know// that's what I'm slowly coming to be able to live with// the fact that it was both, he was a lying shit and he was a loving partner, and people are a complicated mix//*

10. *... living in remote places// not seeing people very much// did maybe eight months of counseling// definitely difficulties still// I think time is the biggest thing isn't it// mountain trips// they've been really healing but// it was something we'd do together// so those things are kind of double-edged in lots of ways// often find them quite emotionally charged// amazing and necessary and difficult at the same time// done interviews and helped... and those things have been cathartic// always thought I wanted to do my own writing, we spoke about this didn't we// seem to still not be doing it// when I talk to someone else I feel like I get release and then I don't have to follow it up// would have to go back in there// there was working on that play that was really helpful// guess that is a therapy, you do get drama therapy, people get to play out their// talked to the writer a lot// the script went backwards and forwards and I did a lot of editing// it was helpful and expressing something but there was*

safety in the fact that it was fiction// didn't have to represent the story// after I'd seen the performance it felt really weird to leave// really torn between never wanting to sit through it again, and wanting to go every night// maybe I could get a job selling ice-creams// wanted to overhear what people were saying about it// weird going to the toilet in the interval and hearing people talking about it// felt really validating// people coming out and saying oh my god I can't believe that really happened, you know people saying stuff like that//

11. *... institutions that don't give a fuck about the humans that work for them and the humans that are not working for them// everyone just collateral// yeh they had that phrase, collateral intrusion// who counted as collateral intrusion and who counted as legitimate targets// saw some documents from one of the court cases that collapsed// some were Marks notebooks// some were all the authorisations for various things that he was going to// he always said I tried to keep you out as much as possible// not sure if that was concern for me or covering his own back/// we still don't know if he was officially authorised to be in a relationship with me or not// I suspect, I don't know how they can possibly have not known, I'm sure they knew// when you look at all those authorisations// there'll be a few throw away comments that will be massive to me// authorising him to stay in for longer// to go home for some leave, and you know the timings of all those things will be significant to me// 'we're not monitoring him over the weekend, we're monitoring him again on Monday'// 'going to an activist event'// a wedding// mentions everybody there is likely to be of a 'similar activist background'// likeminded, therefore there is 'no issue of collateral intrusion' // basically everybody at the wedding was fair game// thing about collateral intrusion in relation to his neighbours// used to invite him round for dinner// had to apply specially for authorisation to hang out// because they weren't anything to do with the targets// basically these people are being intruded on by this police operation but other people are deliberately being intruded on// allowed to hang out with these people but not allowed to report about them, not passing back any information about their private lives // I think about when he came to my Dad's funeral// in the funeral car with my cousin// was my cousin not collateral// maybe they were, maybe I'll see a file one day that mentions that*

day, and which family members were fair game and which ones were not//

12. *... a common dynamic// not being able to plan things with him// then all of a sudden he'd ring up and say oh actually I am free next week// obvious now, it always felt like we weren't planning our lives together// realising for all those years you didn't have free will// you think you're negotiating with your boyfriend about whether he's working or coming// actually there's a series of files, authorisations and people that need to be consulted that you have absolutely no idea about// shaping the day to day direction of your life// that's the thing that makes it different from just somebody who was really married with kids// institutional// and just not knowing how much they watched// I dunno, in a room down the road that he would be able to report or escape to really easily, or they'd be able to see what was going on// how many times was it like that// how many times was it that he was just being left to it// just needed to give them a general sense of what he was doing// how much would he report back// it's that kind of stuff that I'll never know// a bit of me that thinks maybe if I asked him now, maybe he's less// dunno// don't think there's ever going to be a time where he's not covering his back// sometimes think I could seek him out// for ages it was almost like I just want to go and observe// just want to go and see, do I recognise him// is the person that I knew, is that him or is it really not// are you just some arrogant wanker or were you the person that I thought I saw//*

13. *...I want to see all the files// that's been the request of everything I've done so far// having said that, as time goes by I kind of feel less of a strong need// think it will always be significant// also I just think — it is their tactic — I am feeling ground down// all the bureaucratic hearings// directions// debates// not that anything came out of our personal court case that was significant// we got that apology// limited value really, they just said what they needed to say to save face in public// didn't really mean anything// don't feel like there's been any examination of those people who were maybe watching him// directing him// he was reporting to// who was he popping out to have a word with// ringing// how much about me did they know// how much about me did they actually watch//*

14. *...he had this character who he called Uncle Phil// I remember reading something// how they always picked a family member or a character and gave them a name when actually they were referring to their handler// it was often Uncle// I remember Mark talked about his Uncle Phil// how Uncle Phil used to feel a bit sorry for him// used to give him a bit of work// he would go and stay with his Uncle Phil, or go for Sunday dinner and I remember saying, which one of us are you embarrassed of// why can't I meet Uncle Phil, are you embarrassed of him or are you embarrassed of me// he would always say Uncle Phil was a bit embarrassing, how Uncle Phil was this rich capitalist guy and we wouldn't get on// often used to borrow things from Uncle Phil// vans// think he borrowed a projector from Uncle Phil once for a climate camp// who was Uncle Phil// what role did those people have, how close were they, how physically close were they as well as emotionally close//*

15. *... yeh, there's so much to say// I have no idea like have I said all the things, or have I just said some of the things//*

I believe that the facts stated in this witness statement are true.
Signature: ————
Date: —————

Out of this World
for Soraya

This is our chance to get the world excited about space again
— Mars One applicant

1. Mars One

What is the likelihood of this coming to pass?
There is a question about viability.

And how many people applied?
They say around 200,000.

And how many will be shortlisted?
10 groups of 4.

And when will they be leaving?
2027.

How long will the journey take?
Between 7 to 8 months.

And will they return?
No, they will die there.

And how will they survive?
They will grow their own food.

And who are the funders?
Reality TV.

And who will be watching?
People in front of their televisions.

And why are you asking?
Because I need someone to help me.

2. Landing back, June 15th 2016

The wide Kazakhstani plains, the charred shuttle that seered its way through the atmosphere, and crouched, sweating in metal-looped space suits them landing, muscle and bone density mass so sparse, inner ear a-skew, they are carried in chairs across the grasses. Medical teams and journalists surround, he is saying he feels *fantastic*, a weak thumbs up, his pale, thin skin, not sure he can see so well, his eyesight blur all that cranial pressure at zero gravity, six months gazing down at the earth and back, *don't forget to look behind you* they told him *into all the darkness and the stars*

Someone from the press calls *Tim, how are you, how do you feel?* And, seated, a nurse wiping his re-entry sweat off his face in the sunlight, and feigning solid in such crazy disorientation, he tells us *Just truly elated... I mean just the smells of earth are so strong... it's just wonderful to be back... the fresh air is lovely.*

3. Heaven

It'll be us interlocked fingers
and woven into each other

            limbs and skin

warm by that fire in the
sweet heather

taking the night sky in to us

The galaxy ours
the milky way turning   Jupiter
heraldic in Virgo

the long swing
            all the wandering ones
constellated in our favour
            shooting stars
            in the Pleiades
            burning out

60 miles up

meteor showers in Perseus, the Plough
marking hours
circling the pole star
clock

There will be a moon waxing in Cancer
then the dawn come in the east —
whitening out, cool

bringing us back down,
damp dew
the embers
glowing red — the daybreak streak
bleeding the horizon
as the sun fires up
and we know it will be another hot day

and we will swim together

floating on our backs
like starfish

Fire
after Chrystos

I'm licking the salt off
this beat   pulsing in me
both hunger
& hope

all the freedoms hard fought for
everyone who came before me
my gratitude

I'm saying my prayers here
    making my offerings

My mouth shape
the arches of your feet
trace your   bones
ankles
the   inside
of your thighs
breathing   every
part of you   deep
          into me

This is play like cubs
  at your armpit
at the tendon's edge, my lips
at the soft hair & hollow
tracing a circle
at the centre
    of my palm
          over your nipples
    hard up against my hand
          like buds

You make my collapse
    all fire then water
my mouth's
drug   suck   & your long slow

outbreath

The light pales on your breasts
sloping to sternum

I'm pressing
into your ribcage

plunging
into your hips

holding   you   down

Joy
joy
rise you up

sweating
make joy with you
from the tissue in my throat
ululating tunnel
raking my fingers
down the folds of your back
leaving   marks

The sun's rising   it's dawn
I'm anchoring
into the flesh of your ass
weaving my elbows
through your
soft legs

trailing to the waters

to drink

You are fresh
the taste of ozone, blossom
the sea come in   rush

making to you inside now

like a dream world/ sensate

all of my
whole hand
in you

rocking

Vulnerable Hearts

We've stuffed all the soft furnishings
with self-help books to recline on
but when we sleep
we still dream about
the mother love
we might have liked to have had
or the father who wasn't
or the grandfather
possibly
if it is possible to look back
from this knowing place and wish

Vulnerable hearts
we hold them up to each other
look this is my one, look this is mine
dancing around our woundings
and our power
opener of scars
and halls of mirrors

A voice there says
hold the cup steady
be brave
beware spilling
into small tenderness
old pain or muddled hunger

A voice there says
bare yourself
be generous

Guidance — In the Dreaming

I am treading wet
tunnels Underground there are limestone lakes
I am swimming with great ease in illuminated
rivers I am floating down stream dark
like an oil painting in a coracle
the shape of a walnut shell How the
dead come to me here my dog
and now my father They come to me
in a panic of neglect that I
have forgotten to wash or feed them
or I see they are just
fine that they are busy and do not
need me any more

Guidance — On the cards

/Seedplanter
the sky wide open
tending to matter —
at your feet the fertile soil

/Further your talents
all challenges, disappointments
a source of Strength
— you are learning
equilibrium
shift and flux —
let go what is no longer
needed

/Boldness lies ahead
Swords cut through excess

/Let insights serve you
Let courage be yours
Begin

/An intimate
renewal this
of commitment
to love, a force with others
high hope in that deepening

/A hand holds
a yarrow stalk, a staff of wood
(upright) speaking of triumph
Be consistent
Be assured, pace yourself
accordingly, follow through
to completion

/Trust
as you embrace the end
of a cycle, that a new one is
Beginning
Begin

/Faith

Patience
There is suspension, unknown
Yield — to transition, to clear
clean air sweeping away
the old

/Be still
Listen. A feeling of non —
resistance
Bathe yourself in it

/An adventurer stands
on a sandy beach

looks seaward
draws breath

Guidance — Observation

One for sorrow, two for joy
three for a girl, four for a boy
five for silver, six for gold
seven for a story that's never been told

They are scrying in holy wells, in mirrors, tea leaves
coffee grounds, wine sediments, in dust and flour

I am in the park. I have questions
a pair of blue Jays
are shrieking in the treetop

They are casting stones and shells, they are counting thunder
dropping wax in water, striking copper bowls

I am in the park. The following day
the Jays are separate now
and they're silent, one in each tree

They are dowsing with rods, pendulums, observing the patterns in ash
and soot and smoke, they are reading the peat in the black house roof

I walk outside the city. Some time later
a small fledgling blue Jay fallen from its nest
is lying dead in the path

Guidance — As above so below

Just tipped past full moon
the fever-leash that raises
us fluid volume and song
the great revealer —

We can take knowing
from the knowing field
in this waning time

Ancient silver one
speaking us
to ourselves
within wide arcs, orbits, ellipses
Mercury conjunct Mars
Sun trine Saturn

Each aspect and vibration
fortuitous — auspicious
Listen
today may be a good day

And the outer planets
slow roll through the galaxy
how they cast us as generations
lots, straws, if we are lucky
luck

… for the music

an endless Finnish road in the middle of forest, my pa's old Mercedes Benz and this song playing from the stereo

helped my father recover from years of drug and alcohol addiction

My father was so supportive of us. But in my teens I drifted away from him. When I was 17 he passed away due to Cancer. This song really cuts so deep because of all the regrets of not being there

…weekends at Whitby with the lads, freedom from care youthful energy, never ending laughing. what happened? just a old miserable git now

dam i feel old, this was popular when i was like 14… almost 44 holy crapola

can't get home as often presently as I would like and time is going by and people are getting older

Five minutes and forty four seconds of remembering exactly what it meant to be a young boy. And time still passes as I watch… bittersweet. Thank you, music

always been a favorite for me, it's bittersweet though, my husband passed on in November so it's hard as hell right now just putting one step in front of the other

I used to lie awake as a small child listening to my Mum playing this song… Last time I had this played was at her funeral just 3 weeks ago

mother......... I can almost hear you singing.. RIP! Missing you and loving you always!!

me & my mate would sing this at karaoke nights, we went to Afghan together and he took his guitar on our Vehicle he would play this all the time and we would tell him to knock it off! Two years later we went back to Afghan and he was killed, at his funeral we demanded this song. Makes me choke every time, miss you Nigel My Mate, My Comrade and My Brother rest easy

many, many years ago I got the album for Christmas. I would sit in the living room with only the lights from the Christmas tree and listen over and over

as a Catholic boy aged 16 who suffered from clinical depression, this song gave me a demented but satisfying comfort. I played it over and over

I remember as a child in rural England listening to this on the radio and I knew then this song would reckon heavily in my life

I so love her. My husband is deployed right now and I can blast her music anytime right now. She makes me feel things that I have forgotten about myself

That should of been given a standing ovation, not a polite hand clap. What's wrong with these people

When I was a teen, driving alone on a deserted Detroit street in the Winter, many years ago, this was not a good time in my life. I was depressed and lonely. On came this piece on the car radio… The tears came and I had to stop the car. It was a defining moment in my life, a gift from a man who never knew what it would mean for me

I am in tears...my life is at a turning point. Just need the courage to cross the bridge. This music is my refuge

Went outside one night and had this playing with headphones on and looked up and it was a clear night sky and as my eyes adjusted I started to see more stars and more, and this song and seeing all the stars made me feel incredible. Idk what it was but now I look forward every night there is a clear sky

My wife and I played this album on loop in our bedroom for about 2 months at night while our newborn son slept in our bed. It is peaceful, it is beautiful, it is amazing. Thank you

This song makes me think of flying over puget sound in the morning from the water, over the marina, over the train tracks, and it would show the city waking up, pike place starting up…its nice

Play this when you are running over Shooters Hill on a cold winters evening and all of a sudden the whole of London lies beneath you

Try it on a motorbike going out of town

Saturday morning, I haven't slept, but this makes me feel I'm sleeping inside

i feel like a paper boat on a river

Sadness, but in a good way

just drifting with my eyes shut, respect

this is the level of silence I have been longing for all the time

...all of a sudden there is snow outside

tuesday morning, 2am… good enough

Ambulance

You know —
how everyone
manages
to clear a space
in the road
together

Endnotes

Knowledge Rooms —
A friend asked me to cover a yoga class while he was away. Something interested me at the time, in uncharacteristically, simply saying yes. It wasn't til too late in the day to cancel, when I had the company name and address in my hand, that I looked at the Norton Rose Fulbright website and saw the heinous business they were up to. I ran the session, and donated the payment for it to an anti-fracking campaign group in the Southwest.

London Bridge is Falling Down —
Written on the day of the attacks at London Bridge, 3 June 2017

Southwark Cathedral —
Stew — old term for a brothel.
NB *Winchester Geese*, old term for female sex workers who were licensed by the Bishop of Winchester

Home —
Beating the bounds is an ancient tradition, continuing in some places today, where a community walks the boundaries of the parish to share the knowledge of where they lay, and to pray for protection and blessings for the lands.

Forced Swim Test —
Current animal testing called the Forced Swim Test is used to measure the alleged efficacy of what get called anti-depressants. It's modelled on tests Curt Richter did on rats in the 1950s, measuring the effect of feelings of hope or hopelessness in rodents made to swim in jars without escape.

Sleep cycle —
Darkness — "…the bards would compose their works by lying on their backs for a day in a darkened room, with their woven woollen plaids or mantles wrapped around their heads, eyes covered, and a stone on their bellies" p.69 *Soil & Soul* by Alastair McIntosh
Second sleep — There are records that in pre-industrial time sleep patterns didn't involve one block of sleep of a certain number of hours, instead that there was the first and second sleep, with a passage of wakefulness between the two called *the watch*.
Deprivation — Distilled from a youtube interview about sleep deprivation

experiments with Tony Wright.

Spell for Malic, age 2 —
I wrote this poem after a few days of giving massage to women in the camp at Calais. After I'd massaged one woman, she lay her 2 year old (who had been watching intently from the side of the bed) between her legs and I massaged her too. This poem is for her.

Savile/Harris —
In January 2013, a joint report by the NSPCC and Metropolitan Police stated that 450 people had made complaints against TV and radio personality Jimmy Savile, with the period of alleged abuse stretching from 1955 to 2009 and the ages of the complainants at the time of the assaults ranging from 8 to 47.
In 2014, at the age of 84, cartoonist and entertainer Rolf Harris was jailed for 5 years and 9 months on twelve counts of indecent assault on four teenage females during the 1970s and 1980s.

Question —
Syndrome — Asperger was an Austrian pediatrician, medical theorist, and medical professor. He is best known for his early studies, mostly concerning a condition he termed autistic psychopathy (AP). Asperger syndrome (AS), was named after him. Both Asperger's original paediatric diagnosis of AP and the eponymous diagnosis of AS that was named after him several decades later have been controversial, especially since it was announced that under the Nazi regime Asperger sent children to the Am Spiegelgrund clinic, which was set up as a collecting point for children who failed to conform to the regime's criteria of "worthy to live".
Cowgirl — Temple Grandin is an American professor of animal science, consultant to the livestock industry on animal behavior and autism spokesperson. She's one of the first individuals to publicly share insights from her personal experience of what gets called autism.

Casting back —
parsley sage, rosemary and thyme — from the traditional folk song 'Scarborough Fair' — I was once taught a Swedish folk song that listed herbs and told there was some speculation that when common knowledge of abortifacients was repressed and had to go underground, that information may have been passed on in song form.
across the foam — a lyric from a song by the Irish folk band Lankum, referencing all the women who had to travel to get a legal abortion. I saw the

band speak about and play this song just a few days after Ireland repealed the 8.
striking en masse — In 2016, 30,000 women went on strike in Poland to protest a proposed amendment to the already restrictive abortion laws.
Black Friday — demonstration in Poland in 2018 against the attempt by the ruling conservatives and the Catholic Church to ban most abortions.
green pañuelos (bandanas) are the symbol of the National Campaign for the Right to Legal, Safe and Free Abortion which started in 2005 in Argentina.
precious life — anti-abortion campaign group in Northern Ireland.
fetal heartbeat — Legislation has been passed in Iowa, USA, that bans most abortions after a fetal heartbeat is detected, at about 6 weeks into a pregnancy — often before many women even know they're pregnant.
* nb During the Middle Ages the soul was only said to enter the newborn at the time of the *quickening* ('quick' meaning 'alive') — when the first movement was felt in the womb, usually between 16 and 25 weeks.
Roe v. Wade — Landmark decision issued by the United States Supreme Court in 1973 on the issue of the constitutionality of laws that criminalized or restricted access to abortions.

Good sport —
August 2011 — started as protests in Tottenham, London, following the death of Mark Duggan who was shot dead by police on the 4th of August.
August 2012 — London Olympics, which took place at a monetary cost of £8.77bn.

New Clear —
Title inspired by the track 'New Clear Daze' from the album T*he Weather-men Shrug their Shoulders*, by The Ex.

Make no bones about it —
In Japan the family of the deceased perform a bone picking ceremony which occurs after the body has been cremated. Some of the bones remain partially intact. In British crematoriums the bones are ground to 'dust' in a machine called a cremulator.

Manna-hata —
It is said that *Manhattan* is derived from *Manna-hata*, a Dutch colonisers version of a Lenape place name. I have read that the original place name comes from the Munsi language of the Lenape, possibly meaning *island of many hills*. Other theories say that it comes from one of three Munsi

words. *"Manahactanienk"* meaning *"place of inebriation"*. Other possibilities are *"manahatouh"* meaning *"a place where wood is available for making bows and arrows"* and *"menatay"* meaning *"the island"*.

Öngtupqa —
When I visited the Grand Canyon as I was passing through Arizona, I was just there for a fairly brief time at the rim. At the time I was only aware of references to the Hopi salt trails and so used the Hopi name for the Canyon as a title for some words. It's only subsequently that I've learned more. As I currently understand it the Grand Canyon is a culturally important place for several tribes in the Southwest and is described as the place of emergence for the Navajo, Hopi and Zuni. The Navajo name for the canyon is Tsékooh Hatsoh, "rock canyon of great space" and the Hopi name Öngtupqa means "home of the ancestors," or "final spiritual resting place" and initiation ceremonies have passed on specific knowledge and training needed to enter Öngtupqa without incurring spiritual danger. The legacy of brutal colonial violences, and the fact that millions of people are drawn to visit, means a huge volume of people continue to enter the Canyon. Hopi pilgrimages to the Hopi Salt Mines have been taken for more than a thousand years as part of a ritual initiation for Hopi young men. There are no doubt various feelings held by indigenous peoples about visitors to the canyon, but a request I have read repeatedly is that if you choose to enter the canyon, you show respect and treat it as the sacred location that it is, that you leave archaeological/sacred sites as you find them, and that you don't go to Sipapuni or the Hopi Salt Mines (Öönga).

Faultline —
Reference given to the distopian novel *In the Country of Last Things* by Paul Auster

Ahwahnee —
As I currently understand it the Awahnechee are a Miwok people who traditionally lived in the region around and in what is frequently called Yosemite Valley, which they knew as "Ahwahnee," or "gaping mouth-like place" because the valley walls resembled a gaping bear's mouth. It is only since visiting that I have learned that during the Mariposa War in 1851, California soldiers expelled the Ahwahneechee and renamed the valley "Yosemite", a word derived from the name of one of the tribes of people who lived there. The few Ahwahneechee allowed to return had to work humiliating jobs entertaining tourists as "Indian performers" to remain in their homeland. The national park finally evicted the last of them

and burned down their remaining homes in a fire-fighting drill in 1969. It has been cited that the conservation movement (and its problems) began with the 1864 Yosemite Grant Act. Conservation leaders like John Muir believed that the indigenous people who had inhabited Yosemite for at least 6,000 years were a desecration and had to go. Citing their hunting techniques that yielded a good living without wasted effort, Muir deemed them "lazy". The process of the two visits I made, to here, and to the Grand Canyon (above) and further reading afterwards has been a reminder to learn more fully about specific indigenous lands and places before considering visiting.

Foot Clinic, Catholic Worker, Skid Row, LA —
I had the amazing privilege to travel in the States with the inspirational Lorna Mauney-Brodeck in her Herb Bus which provides free herbal medicine and foot care clinics for homeless people. herbbus.org

Herman Wallace —
In remembrance of Herman Wallace, one of the Angola 3 who spent 41 years (1972-2013) in solitary confinement. Herman's direct speech taken from the documentary film 'Herman's House'.
For information about prison abolition, prisoner solidarity, protest against prison expansion, IPP and solitary confinement in the UK: prisonabolition.org

Troy Davis —
Prosecution — excepted from a public conversation with Angela Davis: *Bigger Than Incarceration: Angela Davis Talks Mass Criminalization, Mental Health and the War on Drugs*
Reform: France 1789 — *The breaking wheel* — a form of torture where bones were dislocated and the body pulled apart on a wheel. *The Maiden* — an early form of guillotine used between the 16th and 18th centuries as a means of execution in Edinburgh, Scotland.
Last Poets — quoting Abiodun Oyewole, Southbank Centre, London November 2016

Justice for A —
The London Campaign Against Police and State Violence website: londonagainstpoliceviolence.wordpress.com

Uncle Phil —
Words distilled from a recorded personal conversation. The exchange, and

words as they appear here, just touch on some of the issues involved. For a wider overview: https://policespiesoutoflives.org.uk/our-stories/lisas-story

Out of this World —
Mars One is a corporate project aiming to establish a permanent human settlement on Mars. Several unmanned missions are planned, establishing a habitable settlement before carefully selected and trained crews will depart.

Fire —
With thanks and respect to Chrystos, a Menominee self-educated writer and two-spirit activist who has published multiple books and poems that explore indigenous Americans's civil rights, social justice, queer power and feminism.

Guidance — **Observation** —
The children's rhyme about Magpies stands as a legacy of older practices: Ornithomancy (modern term from Greek ornis "bird" and manteia "divination"; take omens from the flight and cries of birds), is the practice of reading omens from the actions of birds
Scrying, also called 'seeing' or 'peeping' is the practice of looking into a medium to detect significant messages or visions. NB "…the accomplished female bard, Maighread Ni Lachainn, would 'see' her poems running along the green turfs that formed the intersection of wall and roof in her blackhouse" p.72 *Soil & Soul* by Alastair McIntosh.

… **for the music**—
unedited comments left under YouTube videos

Acknowledgements

Versions of some poems have been published in International Times, Magma, Long Poem Magazine, and recorded as part of Claquer and Lavender Hex.
For more info, or to get in touch: lisafannen.uk
Cover photo — Soraya Bishop.

Massive thanks Helen Moore, this wouldn't have come about without so much of your amazing encouragement and dialogue, thanks for all the support and creative, political and spiritual solidarity. Also for years of friendship and for being kin, for spiritual, political and creative succour, for casting critical eyes over words and for totally invaluable editing input, for cover design, cover tweaks, legs-up in the basement, having me hitch rides and incredible experiences with you, for time together pulling out the 'old and new testament', for energising exchange in sessions at the poetry school, for collaborations with text and sound, for soul food and adventure — big big thanks and love Jer Reid, Cloudberry MacLean, Natasha Stilwell, Penny Rimbaud, Andra Simons, Raman Mundair, Andi Butler, Deshaye Faughtner, Ainne MacLean, Matthew Caley, Lianne Hall, Arndt, Alex Brew, Natasha Swingler, Deborah Ramsay, Annwen Jones, Bec Chalkley, Lorna Mauney-Brodeck and Soraya Bishop. Thanks and love Nicole and Barbara Fannen. Finally big thanks Jon & Marko at Active/Što čitaš? for all the support, layout, printing and distribution.

Time Travel for Beginners

Darren and Jacky Johnson

ISBN: 978-1-914173-05-9

You can contact Darren and Jacky at:
darrenandjackyjohnson@gmail.com

King's Church Warrington Website is:
http://www.kingschurchwarrington.co.uk

Dedication

We dedicate this book to Abi, Manu and Sam
and thank God that we get to travel through time with you.

Acknowledgements

Thank you to Paul and Rach Johnson for the initial proof read of the manuscript and for knowing us so well that you could make sense of some of our long and meandering sentences.

We are thankful for the investment and encouragement of our parents Ron and Audrey Johnson and Raymond and Deborah Hall.

Thank you to the people named in the book who have helped to shape our thinking and practice of how to live as disciples who make disciples.

Thank you to the Leadership Team of King's Church present and past for your love encouragement and willingness to go on the adventure of being Family on Mission together.

Thank you to the people of King's Church who have journeyed with us as we learn together how to live as disciples of Jesus. Thank you for your resilience, flexibility, sense of fun and love for Jesus.

Thank you to Abi Moldenhauer for the art work for the book cover, for more of Abi's art work see https://www.instagram.com/abigail.deborah1/

Thank you to Jan Holdaway for her encouragement and work in helping to bring this book to print.

'Thanks be to God for His indescribable gift,'
2 Corinthians 9:15

Commendations

I'd love every church leader to read this book. With disarming honesty and genuine humility, Darren and Jacky share their personal journey and what becomes the amazing grace story of King's Church Warrington. Shaped in the process of doing life together with others, it's a journey of discovery, growing clarity and renewed vision for every follower of Jesus to become a disciple maker and every local church a community of hope.

Chris Cartwright
General Superintendent, Elim Pentecostal Church

My friends Darren and Jacky are the real deal. They live what they preach. In obedience to a vision of the church inspired by Jesus and His followers they have sought to build church according to the biblical mandate of making disciples who make disciples. This vision, rooted in the past, lived out in the present and which points towards future possibilities is woven around their own story of planting in the North West.

I highly recommend this book to you whether you are leading a church, planting a church, or simply in a church. You will be encourage and inspired. It is stimulus for the mind and food for the heart.

Dr Nic Harding, Director, Kairos Connexion
Director, Together for the Harvest
Founding Pastor, Frontline

Vulnerable, self-aware and committed to people, Darren and Jacky Johnson have overseen the development of a mission-focused church that has made a difference in the lives of so many people in a very ordinary (in the best sense of that word) town in North West England.

This book weaves their story into the story of their church and the Biblical narrative to give us a sense of what is possible in so many other contexts. Many of us think that 2020 saw some things change permanently. This book could help you see what the future for your church could be.

Honest, grounded, biblically earthed, this account of a church in a working class town suggests what could be true for so many other churches. If we are ready to pay the cost.

Dr Neil Hudson, Senior Leader, Salford Elim Church
Senior Associate, London Institute for Contemporary Christianity

Time Travel for Beginners is a fantastic read, full of wisdom from the past, insights gained in the present, and inspiring vision for the future. If you want to learn how to follow Jesus more closely or if you are a leader who is trying to help others live a missionary life that looks like Jesus, this book is for you. Darren and Jacky Johnson draw fresh water from deep biblical wells as they share the practical lessons they have learned in building a disciple-making movement that is reaching the lost and changing their community.

Bob Rognlien
Author of 'A Jesus-Shaped Life' and *'Recovering the Way'*

Contents

Foreword

If anyone wanted to experience time travel it must surely be out of 2020 – the year this publication was written. It was during the pandemic of that period that some said that 'all the building blocks of church as we know it are in the air and we will have to wait and see where they fall'. Others called for 'new wineskins' and, while it is true that flexibility and change must be welcomed and embraced, wineskins must still remain wineskins however new they are. In other words, however church manifests itself, it will always need form and structure. When Jesus fed the 5000 He first sat them down in groups of fifty. Even miracles need to be managed. Structure and spirituality are not mutually exclusive.

What you will read in the pages that follow is a tried, tested and flexible wineskin. Some commentaries on the nature of what church should look like emanate out of sterile academic research and clinical statistical analysis. What you are about to experience in the pages that follow could not be more different. It is a narrative forged through rich pastoral experience and hammered out on an anvil of struggle as well as joy – exactly as the Early Church was. Anyone in any doubt about that might want to read the first chapter of Paul's second letter to the Corinthians.

I have known Darren and Jacky Johnson for more than two decades, and they rate incredibly highly in my estimation of what spiritual leadership should look like. Their heart for people, and their love for the local church, marries strength with vulnerability and confidence in God with a genuine humility. They are people that other people want to follow. I have personally witnessed their journey and I thank God for them both.

One of the many telling phrases, in a book that encourages us to see church to grow in depth as well as size, is *'the past and future shape the present.'* Nothing could be more perceptive or relevant in the context in which we find ourselves in these pivotal days.

I have no doubt that you will be as blessed and challenged as I have been as you read the pages that follow.

John Glass
General Superintendent, Elim Churches, 2000-2016
Chair of Council, Evangelical Alliance, 2014-2018

Introduction

The BBC TV series *Doctor Who* has been a firm favourite in our home. The Doctor, in various guises over the years, has appeared on our screen travelling backwards and forwards through space and time. That would be an amazing thing to do. If you could time travel, where would you go? Would you go backwards or forwards first? How far would you travel? Who would you love to meet? What would you like to discover? What do you want to know?

There are times when I would love to travel back and see the landmark events of history. To see the wonder of the beginning of God's creation. To see the world just how He intended it to be with no pain, need, suffering but with harmony, love and peace. I would be fascinated to see the history of God making covenant with people and His dealings with people like Noah, Abraham, Gideon, Ruth, David, Nehemiah amongst others.

Moving forward, wouldn't it be amazing to be able to be present when the angel Gabriel visited Mary and later at the birth of Jesus? How awe inspiring to be present at the crux of history and to see the life and ministry of Jesus unfold and to be there at His death and resurrection.

As a fan of history the list could go on and on: the incredible spread of the early church as disciples made disciples. The great moves of the Holy Spirit throughout history. The early church fathers, Celtic missionaries, the great reformers and so on.

Not to mention Everton winning the league in 1970, *The Beatles* recording *Sergeant Pepper* and *The Stone Roses* playing Spike Island!

Perhaps we could travel forwards and see just how God restores all things and brings this phase of history beautifully to a conclusion. We could see how technology and space travel would develop. As you can see, I have given quite a bit of thought to this.

My conclusion is that vast leaps in time travel, however desirable, are just not possible. However, we can travel slowly though time moment by moment, one day at a time and, in those days, we have the invitation and challenge to increasingly become the people that God invites us to be. We do not travel alone; He is with us and He knows completely the past, present and future. He is our guide and He speaks to us about the future, distant and near. He helps us to make sense of the past without being limited and defined by it. He also gives us the grace that we need to live today. Like 'The Doctor', we do not travel alone. He places people with us and only together with them do we get to be all that God invites us to be.

So, this book is a snapshot of a journey through space and time. How we make the most of key moments and move, one day at a time, forwards into the future that God invites us to.

Darren

Chapter 1

Endings and Beginnings

It was January 2002 and I found myself sat in a church leaders' meeting that I was chairing. To be honest, I had been in better meetings but then again, I had been in worse. During the course of the evening I found that I was experiencing something quite unusual. I would begin a sentence and by the time I got to the end of the sentence I couldn't remember the start. Very disconcerting. I didn't tell anyone what was happening but asked for a comfort break and went to the gents' loos. I stood at the sink splashing water on my face and telling myself to *'Pull yourself together.'*

The meeting reconvened and I continued to chair it. Later that evening at home Jacky and I talked about the events of the meeting. She suggested that I go to see the doctor the next day. I was not too keen on that idea and so went to bed. Just as an aside, I have spoken to some of the people in that leaders' meeting since and they were totally unaware of what was happening to me. This is a little worrying as it suggests that I make about as much sense when I can remember what I am talking about as when I can't!

Burnout and Breakdown

On the following evening, we had another leaders' meeting with the same group of leaders and I had a very similar experience. Again, I said nothing about it to those present but concluded the meeting and walked home – wondering what was happening to me. Again, I spoke to Jacky and again she suggested that I go to see the doctor the next day. Again, I wasn't too keen on that idea and went to bed. Jacky was clearly more aware of my health situation than I was.

The next morning, I went to the church office as usual and sat behind the desk – I really wasn't feeling good at all. Then this thought came to me, *'Perhaps I should go to see my doctor.'* I called the surgery, made an appointment and later that morning was sat in front of my doctor.

I told him what had been happening to me and how I was feeling. He told me that it would be good if I took two weeks off from my church responsibilities. This was the beginning of January and I explained to him that this is a very significant season for us as a church and that I could possibly fit two weeks off around April time. He explained that he was advising me, as a doctor, that I needed to slow down and rest. I reiterated that I couldn't do that right now but that it may be possible in April. I left his office thinking what a waste of time that had been.

Later that day, when I relayed that conversation to Jacky, she strongly advised me to take some time off. I reluctantly agreed to have a one-week holiday. That is when I really began to unravel.

Over the previous years, due to perfectly understandable circumstances, I had developed some very unhealthy work patterns. It began with seasons of busyness. When the need for that season ended, I found it hard to slow down because I discovered that you can get a lot done if you commit to continuously working long hours. What I didn't realise was that, in the end that will catch up with you. Perhaps it started from good motives, but I am sure there was a measure of ambition and need for approval thrown in there too.

As Jesus was walking from Jerusalem, after the last supper, and making His way over to the Mount of Olives, He was teaching His disciples. Maybe, as He walked through the Kidron Valley and up to the Garden of Gethsemane, He looked back at the Temple and remembered the vine that was embossed over some of the doors. Or, perhaps He was walking though the pilgrims camping on the outskirts of the city, there for Passover, that He passed a vineyard. Whatever prompted the thought, He began to explain that He is the vine and we are the branches. If we abide in Him, we will grow and bear much fruit – then His Father the Gardener will come along and prune us, so that we can abide again and ultimately grow and bear even more fruit.

I had been desperate to bear much fruit but had to learn the lesson of being cut back, pruned and of abiding so that I would bear lasting fruit. Missional Leader and writer Mike Breen helpfully says that, *'The process of discipleship is one of death and resurrection.'* I was about to learn this first-hand.

I sank lower and lower. I began to feel like such a failure. I couldn't speak to people easily and would do my best to withdraw from all but those who were closest to me. From regularly speaking to hundreds of people, I struggled to be with more than two or three people at a time.

As weeks turned into months, I was prescribed anti-depressants and tranquillizers. I would pray and read the Bible each day but struggled to hear God and sense His presence. During this season our house had been up for sale and had sold. Due to my health, I felt unable to view houses and so our family of four found ourselves living in two bedrooms in our relatives' home.

I began to ask all sorts of questions. What kind of Christian am I to end up like this? What kind of leader am I? What kind of husband am I? What kind of dad am I? I felt like I had failed so many people.

My hair was getting longer as I didn't feel confident to go to get it cut. I would go out with Jacky in the afternoon to places where no one would know me and walk around, usually not saying much. In the evenings, I would occasionally go out for a walk in the area where we were staying as I was unlikely to meet anyone that I knew.

Around July time the church leaders, at the church where I was the senior minister, met and decided that things needed to move on at the church. They thanked me for my time with them as a leader and said that I would no longer be the senior minister of the church. I felt completely broken.

I remember one evening walking along the road, where we were living, talking to God. I was telling Him that, as far as I knew, there was nothing left in me holding on to Him. In that moment I sensed God speaking to me. He assured me that it was not that I was holding on to Him but that He was holding on to me. It was such a relief and comfort to hear God speaking.

Healing and Recovery

Around this time a friend of ours from the USA, Marc Dupont, got in touch. He was unaware of all that had been happening to us. He just knew that I had been unwell. He asked if he could meet us as he had a prophetic word for us. We arranged to meet in the side room of a church building in Crewe. Marc said to Jacky that she may want to write down what he was about to say. Then, for about 15 minutes, Marc spoke into our lives. It was as if God had told Him what I had been praying about. As if he had been reading my mail. He spoke into all of my questions and fears. Then he offered to pray for me for healing. I agreed.

As Marc prayed, I gently shook – I don't think that this was a manifestation of the Holy Spirit but just something that seemed to happen when I was nervous. I was not instantly healed but, from that point on, I stopped getting worse and started getting better. Over a period of time in consultation with my doctor, I reduced my medication and, over a period of months, stopped using it completely.

As a family, we found ourselves with no home of our own, no job and no permanent source of income. A few friends who were church leaders invited us to move to the area where they were based to consider being a part of their team, but that did not seem right. My father-in-law runs his own business in Cumbria and he offered that we could go and live with them for a while and work for him. This did not sit right with us either, even though we had our children enrolled to start school in Cumbria that September.

It is so encouraging to remember that one of the names for the Son of God is *'Jesus of Nazareth'*. He was born in Bethlehem, spent some of His early childhood in Egypt and had His ministry headquarters in Capernaum. He died and rose again just outside of Jerusalem and yet, He is called Jesus of Nazareth – why? It is the place of rejection. He was rejected and even considered a heretic in the town where He grew up. In fact, at one point, the townspeople were going to throw Him off a cliff because they believed what He was saying was heretical. There would have been members of His family in that synagogue at the time and we have no record of them trying to stop what was happening to Him.

This must have been a very painful episode in the life of Jesus. However, Jesus lived in the power of the Holy Spirit and did not allow the pain of rejection to shape His future. He set off to build a new *oikos* – *oikos* was an extended family household that included both blood and non-blood relationships – it was a new chapter in His story.

Blank Piece of Paper

The General Superintendent of the Elim Churches at the time was John Glass. John said to us that we now had a 'blank piece of paper'. This seemed very significant to us. This was a new chapter in our lives. We felt broken but also had a growing sense of expectancy of what God might want to do.

Chapter 2

Dressed Stones

Jesus said that He would build His church and the gates of Hell would not prevail against us. Jesus was a *'Tekton'* – a builder. He knew what it was to work with wood and with stone. It is likely that He was involved in the building of many houses and I guess that they were built to an outstanding standard.

He is the one who is building the church. We get to join in. We get be disciples who make disciples.

It was late summer 2002 and Jacky and I were wondering if our blank piece of paper should have a church plant on it. If so, we wanted our children to be fully on board with this. We were given some money for a holiday and so, for the very first time, the four of us went overseas together on holiday to the Greek island of Kos. The plan was to rest, recover, think, pray and discuss as a family about the idea of church planting.

Before we went, we mentioned to my brother and sister-in-law that this is what we were planning to do. Rachel (our sister-in-law) gave us some Bible verses from Isaiah about rebuilding with 'dressed stones'. Apparently, this is a term for cut stones that had been used in a previous building and would now be used in a new one.

We discussed the idea of church planting as a family and Abi and Sam were very much on board. We had not heard the phrase ‘Family on Mission’ yet, but this was really what we wanted to be.

Dressed Stones

As a family we are not very good at sitting on the beach for long periods of time. We like to do something with the day. Jacky and I like to walk and to look at architecture and historic sights. A passion that not all of the family always shared! Whilst on Kos, we discovered the remains of an ancient villa and so went to look around and there, in the building, were the ‘dressed stones’ – stones from a previous building that were significant in the newer one. We took this as a confirmation that we were on the right lines as we prepared to head back to the UK and begin the adventure of planting a church – somewhere…

We were not entirely sure where this church plant should be. Some people suggested a town that didn't seem right to us. Another person suggested going back to the town that we had led the church in and planting a new church there. This certainly didn't sit well with us. One day we went into the nearby town of Warrington and somehow this ‘felt’ like the right place to be. We began the process of looking for a house to rent.

I will never forget the first person who asked to join us in the church plant. A dear friend named Col Jeffs said to me, ‘I believe that you are going to plant a church – where are we going?’ This was such an encouragement to us and a real sign of covenant. Though I have to admit that I do regret not saying to him ‘Baghdad’ just to see how he would respond!

We told him that we were going to move to Warrington to plant a church. Little did we know that Paul and Rachel (my brother and sister-in-law) and some friends, a year or two earlier at

Stoneleigh Bible Week, had felt called to plant a church in Warrington. They had written this down and been thinking and praying about when they should act upon it.

We had the beginnings of a pioneer team. Others, like a children's evangelist Paul Caine and his wife Jeanette, offered to help us too. One day I was walking down the road and someone that I knew pulled their car up next to me and said, 'I believe that you are going to plant a church. I will do your admin for you if you like.' By the time we had our first gathering in our home there were over twenty of us!

I remember, some years earlier, reading an article by Terry Virgo saying that one of the big mistakes that happen in church planting is to go public too early. We certainly did not want to do this. We had no plans to try to attract a crowd by putting on a good meeting. We wanted to plant a church not just run a service.

We firmly believed in maintaining and repairing relationships and so had no intention of leaving the Elim movement to which we belonged. We had a conversation with our regional leader explaining that we did not want a building, money or people but we did want permission to rethink and reimagine what church could and should be like in our area now. We were given permission.

Move to Warrington

So, having rented a house for six months, we began to meet in our living room. We would eat cake and drink coffee together. We would pray and think about how we could reach people with the Good News. Jacky and I would bring some simple Bible input around what we had been thinking church could be like.

We began to discuss what really matters for followers of Jesus. What are the essentials for us to live as disciples? We began to agree that there were lots of things that people said mattered that really don't matter that much. Do we sing ancient hymns or modern songs in our celebration meetings? It doesn't really matter. Do we read from the NIV or the AV version of the Bible? It doesn't really matter. Do we wear suits or jeans and t-shirts for church meetings? As long as you have clothes on, it really doesn't matter! The list could go on and on of things that the church seemed to make into issues that, in the end, we thought were not essential. We began to conclude that there are really not that many things that really matter, but the few things that do matter, matter a great deal.

We concluded that it really matters that followers of Jesus love God and that the longer they follow Him and enjoy being adopted into the Father's family, the more they should grow in love with Him. Sometimes it seemed like people loved God to start with and then seemed to get religious, judgmental or caught up on side issues.

We also thought that it really matters that followers of Jesus love one another. That we have people around us who we share life with and don't just attend meetings with – people who are in covenant with us. People who know and love us and who we know and love. People who feel like extended family and who walk with us through life's ups and downs.

We also believed that it really matters that those of us who are disciples of Jesus, make disciples of Jesus. That we share the Good News with those around us in a way that they can understand and respond to.

What Really Matters: Up, In, Out and ABCDE

We did not have this language at the time, but we came to believe that Jesus lived His life in three dimensions:

- Up – relationship with the Father and the Holy Spirit.

- In – relationship with His *oikos* – His disciples: the three, the twelve, the seventy-two and others.
- Out – the Son of Man came to seek and save the lost. If that is what Jesus did, and we are His followers, then it makes sense that we get to do the same.

We agreed to put it simply like this; 'The purpose of King's Church is to have a deep relationship with God and share Him with others.'

As we held these gatherings in our home, the numbers of people orbiting into them began to grow. We filled our living room, then out into our kitchen and then people would also sit on the stairs that went up from our living room to the next floor of the house. We had done no advertising and had held no public meetings. We were simply building a sense of being a family on mission together.

Over the previous few years Canon Phil Potter, a local vicar who was to become leader of Fresh Expressions, and I had been meeting to pray and have lunch together. I really value those times as they stretched and challenged my thinking. We would discuss what church could be like and what values really matter. Phil really did help to shape our thinking on this stuff.

In recent times Phil has said that, 'Culture eats vision for breakfast.' What we were doing in those early months of King's Church was working out what a discipleship culture could look like. How could we really live with a sense of being extended family on mission?

During those meetings in our home, we began to discuss about what simple values could underpin our three-dimensional purpose.

We thought that it really matters that each disciple of Jesus should discover and deploy their gifts. We called this '**A**ll Involved'.

We noticed that a strange thing seemed to happen in Christianity. People would become followers of Jesus and would get to know the Bible but that did not always equate to becoming more like Jesus. So, instead of their Bible knowledge making them seem more like Jesus, i.e. holy, loving, kind, gracious and truthful; they seemed to be critical, judgmental, argumentative and exclusive. This made us think about the importance of '**B**elieving and Doing what the Bible says'.

We then thought about the vital nature of good relationships within the church family. It really matters that we don't just go for convenient, disposable relationships but that we genuinely see each other as the Family of God – we are in covenant with one another. That means that we are committed to each other when things are going well and when they are not. That we will speak the truth in love to each other and we will forgive each other. We certainly have not always got this right, but it has been so encouraging and inspiring over the years to see, in all our imperfection, a group of people learning to live this way. A '**C**ommunity of committed relationships'.

It seemed to us that all Christians seemed to think that evangelism is important and that someone should be doing it. We were even willing to pay people to do this for us but what we noticed is that many, if not most, Christians do not find actually doing evangelism easy and so try to avoid it. We wanted to be clear from the beginning that evangelism is important to us and so our fourth value is '**D**isciples making disciples'.

I am so glad that we nailed that in the early days, and we have needed to keep coming back to this and re-emphasizing it. I remember a conversation with a couple who were thinking of joining King's, in the early days, who told me that they enjoyed the worship and the teaching but that we needed to be more prayerful (fair point) and that we needed to maybe dial down some of the evangelism. I explained that we were just getting started as a church and we knew that we still have lots to learn. However, if they didn't like the level of evangelism and mission now, they would hate it in a year's time as we only intended to increase it!

Our fifth value that we settled on, in those early days, and that we still hold to is – '**E**mpowered by the Holy Spirit'. We believe that we can only really live the life of a follower of Jesus, in the way that Jesus lived His earthly life, if we live in the power of the Holy Spirit. Being a disciple means following the words, works and ways of Jesus. He lived in the power of the Holy Spirit, so we get to do the same. It is the Holy Spirit who assures us that we are children of God. It is the Holy Spirit who gives us gifts to use as followers of Jesus and it is the Holy Spirit who gives us the courage to live as disciples who make disciples.

We had not held a public meeting, rented a venue, done any advertising or gone public yet but we were becoming a family on mission and God was adding to our number. We were working out what it would and could look like for us to follow Jesus together. We had not really explored how all of this could be structured yet, because we believe as Erwin McManus, the author, and lead pastor of Mosaic, a church based in Los Angeles says, that 'structure supports life – it does not create life.' We were very clear that we did not just want to hold a meeting. We wanted to be a church, living as disciples of Jesus each day.

Chapter 3

Who Gets to Join In?

A – All Involved

We have often said that, if King's were a ship, it would be more of a battleship than a cruise ship. On a cruise ship there is a staff team or crew who do all of the work and everyone else sits back, enjoys the ride and is served.

There is such a strong sense of consumerism in our culture that people can often approach church this way. They rate the music, children's work, youth provision, preaching and even the coffee! If all of this meets their requirements, then they come on board for the ride – a cruise ship.

On a battleship, everyone has a part to play. They have a strong sense of team – even family. They all work together, eat together, have time off together. There are no passengers and a vital job gets done – that sounds more like church as it should be.

A snapshot from ancient history – Nehemiah

Israel had really drifted away from God to the point where they had ignored His constant warnings and pleas, through the prophets, to return to Him. So, the point came where they had to face the consequence of their actions and they went into exile. For a time, they had to leave land that had been given to them by God – but God promised that they would be back.

The Bible books of Ezra, Haggai, Zechariah and Nehemiah tell the story of that return. Nehemiah had a job in the palace of the king where he was in exile. He was cupbearer to the king. Sounds good but it was a bit of a dangerous job. You see, the kings in those days faced real threats to their lives and often people who wanted a regime change would go about it by poisoning the king and killing his family. So, the cupbearer got the job of tasting all the food and drink that was given to the king to make sure that it wasn't poisoned.

Nehemiah would ask visitors to the palace about how things were going back in Jerusalem. He would pray for the city, the nation and the people. One day his concern was so great, because he had heard how bad things were back in Jerusalem, that he was sad in the king's presence (Nehemiah 2:1-8). This sounds like no big deal but, in those days, that could not only lose you your job but your life! You thought your workplace was a bit harsh!

The king asked Nehemiah about why he was sad. Remember, he had been praying for Jerusalem, the nation and the people. When we pray, God often gives us the opportunity to play a part in being the answer to that prayer. Nehemiah tells the king about why he is sad and a conversation unfolds in which the king releases Nehemiah, with authority and provision, to do something about the state of affairs in Jerusalem. Just a normal day! He woke up as cupbearer to the king and went to bed as a man charged with the rebuilding of the city of Jerusalem. God sees what is in your heart and, in a moment, can open the way for amazing things to happen if you stay close to Him.

So, Nehemiah travels back to Jerusalem. He rides around the city and gets a clear picture of what things are really like. He talks to the people in the city who have influence and then the work of rebuilding begins.

In Nehemiah 3, we have a list of 42 different groups of people who were all involved in rebuilding the wall around Jerusalem. The chapter gives us an anti-clockwise tour of the city, beginning at the Sheep Gate and then north – east – south and back around to the Sheep Gate again. We go with group after group, working next to each other to achieve a single goal. Can you picture the scene in your mind? There are different sized groups of people working on different stretches of wall; some bigger than others, some right outside where they lived and worked others further afield. A buzz of activity as the work progresses and each person playing their part.

This is a fantastic picture of what God always dreamed of. You see, way back in the early pages of the Bible, in Exodus 19:4-6, God spoke to the Hebrew people and said that He intended them to be *'a kingdom of priests'*. That means that the whole nation would be involved in representing people to God and telling people about this amazing God. However, that is not how it worked out and, in Exodus 20:18, the people wanted Moses to do the job. What they ended up with was a tribe of the Hebrew people who did this, the Levites, instead of the whole nation.

Again, in Numbers 11:29, we see Moses representing what God is dreaming of, when he says that he wishes that all of God's people could speak for Him.

What we see in Nehemiah 3 is a snapshot of what church could be like. Everyone playing a part, leaders leading but everyone serving and the work making real progress.

The prophet Ezekiel saw that a time like this would come. God's dream would be fulfilled when he said in Ezekiel 20:40, *'the entire house of Israel will serve me'*.

In the New Testament, Peter picks this up in 1Peter 2:5, where he tells followers of Jesus that God is building a people and that we are *'a holy priesthood'*. We are to offer *'spiritual sacrifices acceptable to God'*. What on earth are they? Well, things like:

- Romans 12:1-2 – living a life that is committed to doing what God wants and being changed, more and more, into the person that God invites us to be.
- 2 Corinthians 5:20-21 – telling people in word and deed that they can have a living relationship with a loving God.
- 1 Peter 2:9-10 – discovering, developing and using the gifts and abilities that God has given to you.

The people in Nehemiah 3 simply saw that there was a job to be done and a need to be filled and then they did what they could – they all got involved in serving.

One of the great things about Nehemiah 3 is the variety of people involved – one church. Someone that I knew had a poster of Bertie Bassett of the Liquorice Allsorts, outside of his church building, with the statement – 'It takes all sorts to make a church' and it does!

We have Eliashib and the priests in 3:1, used to sacrificing animals and burning incense, now maybe with splinters in his hands from putting the beams in place. In 3:8, we have the goldsmiths, who are used to working with metal and fine detail, now doing a bit of brick laying. I love the fact that 3:9-12 shows us that all kinds of potential divides were broken down. Men and women, young and old, rich and poor, people from the country and those from the city were all involved and working side by side to get the job done.

There are always some who just refuse to get involved – 3:5 tells us about those guys. They were a group of nobles from a place just five miles outside the city called Tekoa who would not *'put their shoulders to the work'*. Maybe it was pride, love of position, indifference – who really knows, but these people would not get involved and it displayed the condition of their heart. When we refuse to serve, it simply displays what is in our heart. Jesus is a servant and so, if we really want to be like Him, we get to serve too. When we flatly refuse to serve, we see where our heart is.

However, it must be said that the vast majority were involved. The phrase *'next to them'* or *'the next section'* occurs again and again in Nehemiah 3. The different groups worked in different areas, building where they were meant to, but they were aware that they were a part of something bigger. What they were building needed to fit in with the people next to them. We believe that every follower of Jesus has a part to play in being a disciple who makes disciples.

We don't do this alone. We are part of an extended family on mission and so we need to be aware of what is happening 'next to us'. We also need to encourage one another as we keep moving forward.

In recent years, we have found the teaching by Mike Breen, Alan Hirsch et al, on the *'fivefold gifts'* in Ephesians 4, to be very helpful. They point out that each follower of Jesus has a 'base gift', listed in Ephesians 4, and that we all have 'phases' where the other gifts are strengthened in us.

> Your base gift is what you can't help but do and
> the phase is what you can't do without help.
>
> Mike Breen

Your base gift is the one that you are most passionate about and the one that refreshes you when you use it. Bill Hybels, the former pastor of Willow Creek Community Church in America, says that our top two gifts, when we use them, usually leave us more energised. The other gifts that we have are still gifts from God but, when we use them, we are often left feeling more drained.

You see, the goal for you as a disciple of Jesus is not to just become an amazing apostle, prophet, evangelist, pastor or teacher; it is to become like Jesus! Ephesians 4 tells us that we need each other and all of the gifts that we bring to help that to happen. So, as evangelists serve with pastors, they learn to care more and as pastors work with evangelists, they learn to risk more in mission. As apostles work with prophets, they learn to hear God better and as prophets work with apostles, they learn to engage with the real process of bringing change. As teachers serve with pastors, they learn to move beyond concepts and see people's needs and as pastors work with teachers, they learn to apply truth that can change hurting lives and so the body of Christ grows up and we, as disciples, become more mature.

It seems to me that, onto the base gift, other gifts are layered. An example would be the way that a teacher may operate in a word of knowledge could be different to how an evangelist may operate in the same gift.

So, God takes us into phases of the fivefold gifts where we seem to be out of our comfort zone, serving outside of our base gift and main passion, so that we can learn from others and become more rounded followers of Jesus. It is in our weakness that His strength is more fully seen.

You will always return to your base gift because that is the gift that you are to the church, but God wants each of us to grow to be more like Jesus in every area of our lives and He is the perfect example of each of the fivefold gifts.

> We are not all called to be pastors, but we are all called to care. We are not all called to be teachers, but we are all called to hold out the truth. We are all responsible for learning how to listen for God's voice, something that comes naturally for the prophet. We are all called to share the Good News with others, but this takes all those of us who are not evangelists out of their comfort zone.

> And we are not all apostles, but must learn to walk out into what God calls us to do.
>
> Mike Breen

So, do you see how important it is to be the person that God has gifted you to be? If you do, you will grow into all that He has for you and you will help others to become more like Jesus as they learn from you too. We need each other and are at our best when we are in community – a family on mission.

The word 'disciple' means 'learner', so do you see how important it is to make room in your life for people with different gifts to you? When you do this, you can grow as a follower of Jesus and your family on mission can be a more accurate representation of Jesus to one another and to the neighbourhood or network that you are trying to reach.

Chapter 4

Do What You Know

B - Believing and Doing what the Bible says

Value **B** at King's is *'Believing and doing what the Bible says'*. This really does impact on how we get to live as a family on mission.

The Bible can be seen in many ways, but here are three:

- Picture – see what is possible.
- Mirror – see what we are like now. Where we are up to?
- Lens – see the world through the view of the truth and therefore gain perspective.

All Scripture is God-breathed and is useful for teaching, rebuking, correcting and training in righteousness, so that the servant of God may be thoroughly equipped for every good work.

2 Timothy 3:16-17 NIV

Therefore everyone who hears these words of mine and puts them into practice is like a wise man who built his house on the rock. The rain

> *came down, the streams rose, and the winds blew and beat against that house; yet it did not fall, because it had its foundation on the rock. But everyone who hears these words of mine and does not put them into practice is like a foolish man who built his house on sand. The rain came down, the streams rose, and the winds blew and beat against that house, and it fell with a great crash.*
>
> Matthew 7:24-27 NIV

So, the Bible tells us that the Bible is useful and, if applied properly, it will make us '*thoroughly equipped*'. Also, we are wise when we not only hear what Jesus has to say to us, but when we ***hear*** and ***do***. We believe that the Bible is inspired by God, that it is without error, that it tells us clearly the truth about God and humanity. We believe that reading and studying the Bible is important but that we cannot stop there. We must act upon what we read. It is not enough to simply read the Bible and gain lots of information. We must allow that information to bring transformation to our lives.

Spiritual maturity is not simply measured by how much you know about the Bible. How is it that you could give a detailed explanation of the meaning of the visions in the book of Daniel, but you are argumentative, rebellious, proud and judgmental and somehow still seen as mature?! I don't get it. You see, I think we are spiritually mature when our lives more accurately reflect the life of Jesus and that happens when we take what the Bible says and, being empowered by the Holy Spirit, put it into action.

I had also been in a setting where, on occasions, it was possible to preach four different sermons on a Sunday as well as other topics in a midweek Bible study. I had begun to question the effectiveness in all of that. Were we just giving people loads of information that they could not remember? Sometimes, I would get to the end of a Sunday and I couldn't remember what I had been talking about! We were providing a lot of information, but not doing well at giving the opportunities to process stuff and dig into what the Bible is saying, which would lead to transformation. We needed shared lives that could help us to know how to do what we were teaching and learning.

So, from those very early days at King's, we have placed a very high value on the Bible. We have taken seriously the injunctions that it is not just amassing information that counts, but lives being transformed into the likeness of Jesus. We plan a balanced diet of teaching each autumn for the coming year. We make notes available each week, with questions that encourage people to dig into Scripture with other people, to be open and honest and to think about how this applies to an ongoing change of life.

We have a structure in place that helps people to have opportunities regularly, in Missional Communities and Missional Households, to study the Bible and to apply it to life change.

In addition to this, we recommend a daily routine of Bible reading. Asking things like, ‘What would this mean to the people at the time?’ ‘What is God saying to me through the passage?’ ‘What do I need to do as a result of this?’

What does the Bible say that helps us to actually be a ‘Family on Mission’?

When we look at what Jesus said (words), and what He did (ways and works), we gain lots of helpful insights on how we get to live as His followers.

When we look at the life of Jesus, we notice that He lived a three-dimensional life, focusing on three great loves, three relational orientations: UP, IN, and OUT.

To say that Jesus lived ‘UP’, means that He focused on His relationship with His Father. He was known for spending lots of time in prayer, and it was His regular habit to go to synagogue meetings and festivals in Jerusalem that were designed to help people connect with God. Jesus had a rich relationship with His Father – in other words, His life had an UP dimension.

Jesus also focused IN. Among the vast crowds that followed Him, He chose twelve to be very close to Him so He could train them and send them out. Jesus spent a lot of time with His disciples; so much so that they eventually became His family on mission! He took them on retreat with Him to invest time in them. By the end of His earthly ministry, their community was as tight-knit as they come. There was a strong IN dimension to Jesus' life.

Of course, there was also a driving purpose to Jesus' life as He moved OUT. Mission defined His entire life and ministry. Just a few of the ways Jesus expressed this were 'seeking and saving the lost', 'destroying the works of the evil one', and 'doing the will of him who sent me'. Jesus' life was defined by missional purpose – His definitive OUT dimension.

So, if we are going to really **believe** and **do** what the Bible says, then our lives should reflect these three dimensions.

> *Therefore, go and make disciples of all nations, baptising them in the name of the Father and of the Son and of the Holy Spirit, and teaching them to obey everything I have commanded you. And surely, I am with you always, to the very end of the age.*
>
> Matthew 28:19-20 NIV

How, as a *Family on Mission,* do we believe and do what the Bible says here?

Jesus' last words before He ascended back into Heaven were to commission His disciples to make disciples, like He made disciples. So, they are to 'teach as He taught them.' It seems that Jesus did this in both formal and informal ways. He set about building an *oikos* – a household of blood and non-blood relatives with His disciples. It is in context of community/family that these first disciples learned how to do what the Bible says.

This would not be unusual as, in Hebrew culture, people would live as extended families. This would often be around a business, such as fishing. The relationship between Rabbi and disciples is similar to these and to the Greco-Roman households. The Hebrews had a saying, *'May you be covered with the dust of your Rabbi'*. The idea was that disciples would walk alongside the Rabbi as he taught them. They would share life and learn so, if you were walking close to your Rabbi, the dust that was kicked up as he walked would be on you. Therefore, the saying means to walk close to the Rabbi and learn from them. Discipleship is the relationship between the Rabbi and the learners.

How do we take these principles and find a way for people to experience them today? Surely, to do that would help people become the people that God is inviting them to be, by **believing** and **doing** what the Bible says? We learn to do this as we study together, fellowship together, pray together, do mission together, worship together and eat together because, in those formal and informal settings, we are learning to do what the Bible says.

Chapter 5

Travelling Companions

C - Community of Committed Relationships

It seems clear, from the New Testament, that following Jesus was never meant to be done in isolation. God has placed us in His family. If we are going to pioneer and take the opportunities that come our way as followers of Jesus, we need to do it together.

The Day of Pentecost, recorded in Acts 2, shows that God's intent, in the outpouring of the Spirit, is the creation of a community of faith. A community where broken people would be restored in their relationship with God, and relationship with others, for the good of the world.

The book of Acts helps us to see the outworking of the implications of the death and resurrection of Jesus. We see that God's intent is not simply to save individuals. If the cross is restricted to only saving individuals, then it takes away from the story of God. The fabric of a Biblical story, which is the creation of the community of faith and the cross and resurrection of Jesus, opens the door for the creation of this community. The outpouring of the Spirit in Acts 2 and beyond is the story of communities of faith being formed.

Tom Wright, the retired Anglican bishop and New Testament scholar, wrote,

> God doesn't give people the Holy Spirit in order to let them enjoy the spiritual equivalent of a day at Disneyland…the point of the Spirit is to enable those who follow Jesus to take into all the world the news that He is Lord, that He has won the victory over the forces of evil, that a new world has opened up and that we are to help make it happen.

While we read in the book of Acts,

> *They devoted themselves to the apostles' teaching and to fellowship, to the breaking of bread and to prayer. Everyone was filled with awe at the many wonders and signs performed by the apostles. All the believers were together and had everything in common. They sold property and possessions to give to anyone who had need. Every day they continued to meet together in the temple courts. They broke bread in their homes and ate together with glad and sincere hearts, praising God and enjoying the favour of all the people. And the Lord added to their number daily those who were being saved.*
>
> Acts 2:42-47

If we see the church as a ***'family on mission'***, this can be very helpful as it is a phrase that works at all kinds of levels: movement wide, local church wide, groups within a church, nuclear family...

So, if we are going to live as a family on mission, this has implications. We tend to see family as more than a weekly meeting where we sit in rows or even in a little circle with a few people talking. Can you imagine a family where mum and dad got the kids together on Sundays and for an hour and a half on Wednesdays and then said they were family?

What could family on mission look like? What does a Community of Committed Relationships look like? How can we be a family on mission?

In the Acts 2 verses, we see orbiting with rhythms of prayer, food, fellowship and shared resources. So, how can we do these things together? Who are we doing these things with regularly? What does this look like in our month? When do we hang out together and have fun? When do we eat together? When do we gather to pray and for how long? How do we do mission together?

Shared life

Since the end of World War II we, in the UK, have seen the breakdown of extended family. We have seen increasing pressure placed on the nuclear family to fulfil all that the extended family used to do, and the strain has been overwhelming. As a result, we have seen the breaking of many nuclear families.

I can remember, as a small child, growing up on a terraced street in the northwest of England having my grandparents, three aunts and uncles and numerous cousins all living on the same street. The children around would play football or *'Bulldog'* in the street on summer evenings and many families would sit on their steps watching and chatting. This was back in 1936 – I am older than I look! Seriously, this was the very early 1970s. I don't imagine there are many streets like that left in Britain today.

Deep down, we know that we need extended family. In the ancient world they called it *oikos* – a mixture of blood and non-blood relatives. We know, from our obsession with soap operas and TV shows like *Friends*, that people long for a larger network of relationships – an extended family, if you will. There are still remnants of this kind of extended family today, so the comedian Peter Kay talks about his *'aunty who isn't really his aunty – a friend of the family!'*

This is more than a new church programme. This is living as a family of missionary disciples together. It has implications for how we use our time, money, home, stuff etc, it's almost as if we gave our life to Jesus!

This is covenant relationship – not just convenient spiritual consumerism. I have observed, over the years, a sort of 'Buffet Christianity', where people move around from one church to another, one preacher to another just to 'get fed'. Here for worship, there for youth work, this preacher for this need and that one for another. This seems to me like watching a soap opera and thinking that you are one of the people in it: a sort of pseudo-community of convenient relationships. One where, when the challenge is too high or the serving feels too much, then off you go move to the next part of the buffet.

We are invited by Jesus into a family, where we are committed to Him and to one another. If we keep our relationship with Him as it should be, we find it so much easier to work on the relationships with other people. We believe that, for true discipleship to take place, we must be in a community of committed relationships.

Disciples Making Disciples

We wanted to be clear from the very start of King's Church, that making new disciples is not just the job of the SAS followers of Jesus but that every one of us is commissioned, by Jesus, to be disciples who make disciples. Rick Warren, the author of *The Purpose Driven Church*, says, 'The great commission is my commission.'

In the mid-1990s, Jacky had a dream. In the dream, she was sat in the main auditorium of the church building where we served, but there was a difference. The whole of one wall was a window. She was drawn to what was happening through the window rather than what was happening in the church service at the time. She says that the church service seemed to be droning on in the background – she thinks that it must have been me speaking!!

Through the window she could see a hill. On the hill were lots of houses, but all the houses were in complete darkness. In the dream she felt a real sense of panic. Then she noticed a lighthouse on the top of the hill. The lighthouse began to shine and, one by one, the lights came on in each of the houses. At this point Jacky had a great sense of relief in the dream. She then felt God say to her that Jesus is the light of the world, but we have tried to just make Him the light of the church!

We are in the world to shine the Good News to as many people as possible, in a way that they can understand and respond to.

We did not then, and do not now, want to only do an 'attractional' model of mission. One where we host events for people to come to, where they could hear the Good News. This is one way of doing evangelism that we value, but there are so many more. It is vital that each follower of Jesus is confident enough to share the Gospel. It is vital that we can share the Good News in the contexts of our daily lives. That we open our lives up to others in such a way that we can live as disciples who make disciples.

Every follower of Jesus gets to be a disciple who makes disciples. Jesus is our example for life, and He shared the Good News with lots of people. In Luke 19:10, Jesus said that the reason He came was *'to seek and save the lost'*. Jesus loves people and at one point in our lives we are all lost. He died for us and we believe that He has committed to us the responsibility of proclaiming, in word and deed, the Good News to people and to make disciples.

Heaven, Hell and the Love of God

We believe that Hell is a real place of conscious eternal punishment and we want to see as many people as possible avoiding ending up in that place, so we need to tell people about Jesus. Our society is playing down the existence of Hell. In his book, *Whatever Happened to Hell?,* John Blanchard quotes David Lodge as saying,

> At some point in the 1960s, Hell disappeared. No one can say for certain when this happened – first it was there then it wasn't.

Many people in the world, and now in the church, don't want to face up to the reality of Hell. They claim it doesn't exist or caricature it as a place of pleasure and parties. It is true for many that the horror of Hell has lost its significance. In fact, the word is now used in a way that strips it of its original meaning. However, *Strong's Concordance* lists Jesus in the Gospels talking of Hell 14 times directly and then there are the other verses, such as Matthew 25:41, where He doesn't use the word 'Hell' but speaks of *'everlasting fire'*. This being the case, we want as many people as possible to hear the Good News and to enjoy a relationship with God so that Hell will never be something that they experience.

We also believe in the reality of Heaven and that people can really be with God forever – Revelation 21:4. Heaven is a real place with activity, joy, involvement and responsibility. When we become a Christian, the power of sin is broken over our lives. When we are welcomed into Heaven, we live free from the presence of sin.

Jesus died and rose again so that people could be with God forever and enjoy His presence. He is the *'tekton'* – the builder and, according to John 14:1-3, He is at work building rooms in His Father's *oikos* so that we can be with Him forever. Our certain hope is Heaven!

Jude 24 is a wonderful verse. It tells us that we will be presented with great joy. My mind goes back to numerous Saturday afternoons in the month of May, watching the FA Cup Final. At the end of the game the winning team, led by their captain, would ascend the Wembley steps. Then, the FA Cup itself, dressed in the coloured ribbons of the winning team, would be presented. The captain would receive the trophy and turn to face the end of the stadium where their supporters were gathered. He would pause and then lift the trophy and there would be massive celebration – 1995 was a particularly good year for me. A trophy won, presented with great joy. There is delight in Heaven when each one of God's children arrive home.

It was July 2005 and I was stood with my brother Paul at Manchester City's ground, listening to the band Oasis. A gift of two tickets had been given to me by the people at King's for my 40th birthday later that year. It was an amazing concert and, at one point, I was stood in the stands near the halfway line looking out at thousands of people stood with hands raised singing, 'You and I we're gonna live forever.' Right then, I had one of those Holy Spirit moments. Did you know that the Holy Spirit attends Oasis gigs, sporting events, shopping trips, school runs and in-fact wherever you go?! As I stood there, I sensed the Holy Spirit remind me that yes, everyone one of these people here at this amazing gig was going to live forever, as is everyone else. The key question is with whom and where will they live forever? Evangelism helps us to live with an awareness of eternity. There is a Hell to flee and a Heaven to gain.

The Apostle Paul tells us, in 2 Corinthians 5:14, that Christ's love compels us to share the Good News. This is a wonderful picture. The word is used only one other time in the New Testament, in the story of the woman with the issue of blood. Jesus is on His way to Jairus' house to heal his daughter. He is surrounded by a crowd and He stops and asks, 'Who touched me?' We know that the woman came forward and acknowledged it was her. Imagine how the disciples felt when Jesus asked, 'Who touched me?' The disciples replied, 'The people are crowding against you,' (Mark 5:31). This is the idea of being carried by the crowd, hemmed in on all sides and pushed in one direction. It's the same word as in 2 Corinthians 5:14 – 'to compel'. When we experience Christ's love, we are compelled to tell the Good News. The Great Commission is vitally linked to the Greatest Commandment, which is found in Matthew 22:35-40.

We also get to live as disciples who make disciples because of the fear of God. 2 Corinthians 5:11 and 1 Corinthians 9:16 tell us this. The Apostle Paul said, '*Woe to me if I do not preach the Gospel'*. Paul was aware of the seriousness of people facing the Judgement Seat of Christ without a relationship with Him and he was aware of his responsibility, as a Christian, to tell others about Jesus.

How do we get to live as disciples who make disciples?

The Bible gives us instances where people who became followers of Jesus invited others to come hear Him share the Good News (for example the woman in John 4). So, there is a place for us to invite people to events where they can hear about Jesus and choose if they want to follow Him.

There is also the Great Commission in Matthew 28 where we, as disciples, are commissioned by Jesus to ***go*** to all peoples everywhere and make disciples. So, we are to not only invite people to come to hear the Good News. We are also to ***go*** and share the Good News wherever people are.

Rich Robinson, Director of *5Qcollective*, once asked the leaders of our church: *'Who does your heart break for?'* That question has lived with us for years.

Jesus tells us to,

> *Go to all people everywhere and make them my disciples.*
>
> Matthew 28:19

This is an amazing thing for Jesus to ask us to do and, for some of us, it can feel a bit scary. However, in Luke 10:1-12 He does give us some help on how to do this. In Acts 16, some years later, the Apostle Paul applied those principles as he was looking for opportunities to make disciples.

He travelled with 'companions' – v6: Paul was not alone. We are 'Family on Mission', where *relationships and responsibility* go together. It is really important that we build a sense of family and it is really important that we reach out to people who do not know Jesus together. It is not 'either or', but 'both and'.

Keep moving – v6-12: Paul and his companions were on the move and open to the Spirit. They were looking for places that were ready for harvest. It really helps if we have our eyes open to where the harvest is ready, and if we remember that it may not be where we expect it to be. Where is the harvest ready around you?

Jonathan Edwards, the theologian and leader from the 1700s, said that,

> …the task of each generation is to see the direction in which the Sovereign redeemer is moving and then to move in that direction.

We are told to *'lift up your eyes'* and see beyond the obvious and connect with what God is doing in His harvest field. God is at work in the lives of people in your community. Where is it time to sow? Where is it time to water? Where is the harvest ready at the moment? How do you know?

Jim Collins, in *Great by Choice*, says to fire bullets and then fire cannon balls. Do some things that will cost you little investment and, where these show signs of breakthrough, invest more.

Moving to multiplication – v13-15: Jesus loves all people. We are to reach out to the last, the least, the lonely and the lost and, when they become followers of Jesus, His family grows by addition. As we do this, Jesus taught us to look for the 'Person of Peace', because they are the key to movement – to multiplication. How do we recognise a person of peace? The story in Acts 16 helps us here. A person of peace is someone who will listen to you. They want to hear what you have to say. So, in this story, Lydia listened to Paul and his companions (v14). This means that we must be saying something about Jesus very early on in our connection with the people that we are trying to reach.

A person of peace will welcome you and open a network of people to you – in v15 Lydia and her household believed. Lydia warmed the spiritual temperature of the group and a person of peace will do that for you, sometimes even before they themselves become a follower of Jesus. They are a gatekeeper to the group.

Lydia wanted to serve the vision that Paul and his companions had. A person of peace will do that too. She used what she had to further their cause. So, she offered her home as a place for them to stay. So often we think that people connect because we serve and they get served. On occasions that happens, but we need to be careful that we don't create a provider/client relationship. We are aiming for family and, in family, you serve and get served. Jesus is our example and in the Gospel accounts we see that He was just as happy having His feet washed, as washing feet.

Use words and deeds v16-18: Jesus told us, in Luke 10, to preach the good news and heal the sick. So here, Paul and his companions share the words and works of the Kingdom. On this occasion, the demonised slave girl is set free.

This can mean, in the context of our mission, we are open to praying for the sick or seeing people encounter the power of God. Some of the young adults from a couple of our missional communities had been meeting to pray for a few hours, on Friday evenings, and then going into the town centre where the clubs are, until the early hours of Saturday morning. They had filmed words of knowledge on their phones from the prayer time then gone and found the person concerned – not a follower of Jesus. They then showed them what they had from God and offered to pray for them. Some of these people really had an encounter with the Holy Spirit there on the streets or in the club.

Heal the sick – this may be praying for healing for someone or it may be observing what is sick in their world and how can you heal it? Where can you help to bring change for the better?

Overcoming difficulty v19-24: We don't need to look for this or try to be difficult in order to get it. Paul and Silas were beaten and put in jail, but they did not give up. They were confident in who God is and, therefore, who they were. Knowing those things gives us confidence in the difficult times not to give up or go for the latest quick fix, but rather to persevere. Knowing that they were not alone, but that they were loved by God and had other followers of Jesus around them, gave them encouragement to keep going with this opportunity – even in the trial.

Dr Nic Harding, Founding Pastor at Frontline Church, Liverpool and Leader of Kairos Connexions, says, *'Never waste a good trial.'*

If you follow Acts 16 through, you will see that they do the same things again. They stay together, look for opportunity to speak about Jesus, look for who welcomes them and will serve their vision. This person – the jailer – opens his family to them and even more people become followers of Jesus.

By the end of their visit to Philippi, Paul and his companions have reached two people of peace and one person who was perhaps – the last, least and lost and, from this, a church was planted. It seems to me that, when we do what Jesus asks us to do, it has quite an impact!

We all get to do this – the great adventure of being disciples who make disciples.

Empowered by the Holy Spirit

> A skeptical, religious attitude is completely contrary to the spirit of the Bible, a book of the impossible, a book of the supernatural, a book of miracles and wonder. In fact you could sum up the spirit of the New Testament age with the words: '*Everything is possible for him who believes*' (Mark 9:23) – not to him who belittles. Beware of a skeptical heart.
>
> Dr Michael L Brown, Apologist and writer

It is clear to us that, if we are going to be the followers of Jesus that He invites and challenges us to be, then we will need to be 'Empowered by the Holy Spirit'. We read in the Gospels and the Acts of the Apostles, how the Holy Spirit took some 'Men of Galilee' with their small town outlook and low expectations, and expanded their vision, raised their expectations, empowered their lives and they then changed their world. As followers of Jesus today, we are still invited to be 'empowered', to be all that we could be and to do what Jesus asks us to do. Acts 2 gives us an outstanding snapshot of what this can look like.

I think that God wants to empower His church and then I would suggest to you that those amazing events, which we read about in Acts 2 and that took place in the church in Jerusalem around 2000 years ago, are not a one off event but a prototype of what God wants to do in towns and cities all over our world. To release us into our culture and into our world to bring hope, love and peace. To bring, and to be, good news and to change the world.

What this looks like in each place will be different, as we see when reading on in the book of Acts, but nonetheless we are invited into this great adventure of encountering the living God and being His representatives to those around us.

Jesus said, in Acts 1:8, that when we are empowered by the Holy Spirit we will *'Be witnesses.'* If you have been empowered by the Spirit, then you are a witness – the question is are you effective or not?

What can we learn from these early followers of Jesus, which may help us to be all that we could be?

After Jesus was raised from the dead, He appeared to over 500 of His followers. We know this because 1 Corinthians 15:3-7 tells us so. Can you imagine being one of those people? You got to see the risen Jesus, to see the nail prints in His hands and feet, you got to ask Him questions and even eat food with Him! You would see Him appear in rooms and disappear. I love how C S Lewis points out that this is not because Jesus had less substance, but because He had more! So, as a stone passes through water in a glass because it has more density than the water, so the risen Jesus can pass through walls! You would also get to hear what He had to say. One of those things that He said was to wait in Jerusalem until they were filled with the Holy Spirit. The Holy Spirit would empower them to do all that Jesus had asked them to do (Luke 24:49).

Over 500 people who have seen the risen Jesus are asked to wait in Jerusalem to be empowered by the Holy Spirit. However, Acts 1:15 tells us that on the day of Pentecost only one hundred and twenty were there. Where were the other three hundred and eighty plus? We don't know! Maybe they went along for a bit and got bored or distracted or afraid or busy but one thing is for sure, they were not there!

Those days before their empowering encounter were very important. They built strong friendships with each other. They dealt with some outstanding issues. They prayed. They did the simple things. They simply did what Jesus had told them to do in Acts 1:4-5, and what He tells all of His followers to do in Hebrews 10:25; they committed themselves to each other and to meeting with each other.

Pensacola

We had the privilege of visiting a church in Pensacola, Florida, in the 1990s that was experiencing an amazing time of growth, where the empowering activity of the Spirit was clearly evident. The church leader told us that, prior to this season of growth and what could only be called revival, they had changed their Sunday evening service into a prayer meeting and had done this for a long time. Attendance dropped. Then, a time of breakthrough came. They linked the outpouring of the Holy Spirit that they were experiencing, back to this commitment to seek God as He had told them to.

When God empowers us with His Spirit, He is simply keeping His promise. God the Father promises the empowering of the Spirit to followers of Jesus in Luke 24:49. Jesus promises the empowering of the Spirit to His followers in Acts 1:5,8. This is the promise given in the Old Testament and Peter explains this in Acts 2:17-18. So, when we ask God to fill us with His Holy Spirit, we are simply asking Him to do what He has said that He wants to do.

What was the effect of this empowering encounter on those early followers of Jesus? *They became very aware of the presence of Jesus with them.* Earlier in the story, the thought of Jesus' departure had filled them with dismay, but now His invisible presence was filling them with joy and peace. *They became very courageous.* Earlier in the story, they were locked away behind closed doors for fear of what people would do, but as they are empowered by the Spirit, they have amazing courage – Acts 4:31.

If you know what God is asking you to do, or to be, but do not have the courage to do those things or the confidence to be that person, then perhaps it is time for you to be filled with the Spirit. Then He can work with you, empowering you to be all that you know deep down you could be. The selfishness and personal ambition that had been so evident earlier, diminishes. These were people who had been pushing for position and prominence but who now were happy to work as a team. *They had a greater understanding of the Bible* – Luke 24:25. Peter had amazing insight, in Acts 2, about the meaning of Old Testament prophecies, as does James in Acts 15.

If you want to get more out of the Bible and then be able to apply it to your life, then I would encourage you to be filled with the Holy Spirit. He is the One who will guide us into the truth and empower us to be all that God says that we can be. *Their words carried great power* – at breakfast time on the day of Pentecost, there were 120 people in the church. By lunchtime that same day, that had grown to 3120! God can do more in a morning than we can do in a lifetime. Acts 2:37 shows us that the words that were spoken in the power of the Spirit had amazing impact.

They had their season of preparation and the amazing empowering experience. However, the truth is we can only really tell if what we experience is God at work by the fruit. What were the results of this empowering encounter? Let's see in Acts 2:41-47,

- Followers of Jesus did what He said – v41
- People were devoted to Bible teaching – v42

- They became covenant people – deeply devoted to each other and to God – v42
- They were devoted to 'the' fellowship – v42
- They were devoted to prayer – v42
- They had a deep regard for how Holy and Powerful God is – v43
- They were active in meeting one another's needs – v44-45
- They met regularly in different sized groups – v46
- They gladly praised God – v47
- They experienced favour – v47
- They kept growing in number – v47

That all looks like good fruit to us. Are those the kind of things that you would like to see more and more of in your life and in the lives of those that you are discipling? If so, these things do not just happen. We all have a part to play – we need to be *empowered by the Holy Spirit.*

Chapter 6

The Journey Inside and Out

We had been meeting in our rented home discussing, praying and thinking about what it would look like to really live like followers of Jesus. The process was aided with a good supply of coffee, tea and cake! As we met, week by week, we grew in number. I think that there were about nineteen people at our first meeting on a Wednesday evening in September 2002. They filled our living room. We noticed that over the weeks the living room was full and so we overflowed into our kitchen. When that was at its limit, people started to sit on the staircase that came down into our living room. This was all by word of mouth, no advertising, no big publicity drive and no public meeting yet. It seems to us that the Kingdom of God appears to grow like a mustard seed – it starts small and takes root and then begins to grow.

I had the words that I had read by Terry Virgo, some years earlier, running through my mind: *'Church plants often fail because they go public too soon.'*

We had reached capacity in our house, so we began to plan for what to do next. We knew that we did not want to lose the dynamic of meeting in homes, but realised that we needed a larger space too. So, we had a two-pronged plan. It seemed that the church in Acts had at least two wings: one in the large public space of the Temple and the other in the social space of the household or oikos. We set out to work out what this could look like in our context with considerably less people.

Whittle Hall

We rented a community centre in Whittle Hall, West Warrington, for our first Sunday morning celebration. We also began to offer a 'non-commitment leadership training' course. This was held on Monday evenings. The 'non commitment' bit was that, by participating in the leadership training, you were not saying that you would become a leader and we were not saying that we would make you a leader. This was a space where we could explore together who was called at this time to lead and help to lead the cell groups that we were planning to open.

At the time, I remember we were greatly impacted by some work that Joel Comiskey, a missionary and author on the worldwide cell group movement, had done for his PhD. He looked at the contributing factors for group growth in churches around the world that had cell groups of various sizes. His top finding seemed to be that, groups where the leader prayed each day for the people in the group grew, and second was that they had a clear sense of vision, which the people in the cell could articulate. There were lots of other helpful things in his work. To put it simply, as we understood it, the top two factors that would contribute to growth were: we would talk to God and we would listen to what He said and do that. Seemed like a very good idea.

Our first Sunday morning in the community centre went well, it was late October and around 50 people gathered. As part of our core team, we had a number of good musicians but we decided not to go for a big band but rather to have one guitar and singer. We simply worshiped together and then left some space for people to share what God had been doing in their lives. During the talk, we had a class for children and for young people. I spoke that Sunday on Psalm 1, about the tree that is firmly rooted and refreshed will grow and bear fruit. The following Sunday, a new local lady joined us and during the time of sharing told us that she believed that she had a passage of Scripture that would be significant for us – Psalm 1. We were sure that God was speaking to us.

Our leadership training took about nine weeks and, when completed, we had enough leaders to start seven cell groups. We divided everyone into cells and let people know which cell they were in. Then we had ‘transfer season’ – a time before the cells started, where people could move cell if they would prefer to be in another one and there would be no offence taken if people moved out of your cell.

Once that season was over, I am pretty sure there were a few moves and I don't think any money changed hands, we closed our Wednesday gathering in our home and started to gather in cells. These were not to be meetings only, but a place where we could live out our values, where we could learn how to do Up, In and Out together. They were to be a network of relationships that met each week in an organised way, but also connected during the week organically. To varying degrees, they seemed to work. They would be our frontline of mission and of pastoral care.

First Carol Service

Meanwhile, our Sunday celebration was going along fine. We planned our first ‘guest service’ – a celebration where we encouraged everyone to try to bring along a guest. We planned a Christmas Carol service. To help with the atmosphere, we decided to meet on the Sunday evening instead of the morning. We booked the community centre and people really did invite friends.

I remember arriving at the venue for the service and finding the doors locked. *'Not to worry, the caretaker will be along soon to open up',* I thought. People were beginning to arrive to get ready for the service, still no caretaker! I had been trying to get him on the phone but, when I called the only number that I had for him, I could hear the telephone ringing inside the building! People were now arriving with their guests. The street outside the community centre was filling with cars – lots of people, lots of guests, children ready to do their nativity, musicians ready to play, me increasingly less ready to preach!

As time was passing, I called Martin Thorpe, a friend and local Church of England vicar to ask if he knew any of the people who ran the community centre to see if they would come to open up for us. He didn't, but he said that we should bring everyone over to his church building. They weren't meeting that evening and we could use it free of charge! This was typical of Martin's generosity of heart. We walked along the street, leaning into cars and telling people where we were now going to meet and that we would be late starting. I did wonder if people might just go home, but they drove to the other venue and waited for us to set up. I remember preaching with a banging headache, but God moved amongst us. I think that two or three people responded to reconnect with God that evening.

I guess that sometimes we can expect everything to go smoothly when God is at work. However, it seems to me that sometimes it is a bit like the very first Christmas – the miracle is in the mess.

Barrow Hall Primary School

Over the following months, our Sunday gathering began to grow and we needed to change venue and so moved to Barrow Hall Primary School, where we stayed for the next few years. The hall seemed so big to start with, but we began to grow again, through our cells and celebration.

It was during this time that a few things seemed to happen in me. One was that I needed to deal with my inner narrative and the other was that we needed to stand firm for the kind of church that we believed God was asking us to be.

The inner narrative – 'Change the tape'

We had now moved from our rented house into a house that we were in the process of buying. To help fund this Jacky was training as a school teacher. Our children had now moved schools to Warrington. Due to her training in other towns, Jacky needed the family car each week day and so I would take Sam, our youngest child, to school on the bus. Abi is a little older and so could walk to school with friends.

Each morning, Sam and I would set off to school on the bus and then to save money, as things were not easy financially, I would walk home. The walk would take around 45 minutes. I decided to use the time to prayer-walk. So, as I walked through the housing developments and past the shops and businesses in the area, I would pray that God would bless and that we would see a harvest in the area. I believe that this was an important time of 'breaking up the ground' in prayer and we have seen people becoming disciples in those areas since.

However, as I walked and prayed, it became clear to me that there was an inner narrative going on in me that was not healthy. I found that my thinking would time travel back to the time of my illness and all of the fallout from that. I would feel so angry and disappointed by what had happened. I had been trying to process it all and found that counselling had helped but there were still some issues of unforgiveness and hurt in me. It was as if, when my mind was in neutral, there was a recording playing rehearsing all of my hurt, self-pity, anger and unforgiveness. I would catch myself thinking these things and then refocus on what I was supposed to be praying about on my prayer walk, but my mind would easily drift back to this unhealthy place.

I can take you to the place, on Cromwell Avenue, where I stopped and stood still – realising again where my mind had drifted to. I sensed that God gave me some real insight in that moment and at that place. He showed me that it was as if my thinking was like an old cassette tape, playing all of this stuff that would damage me and those I loved if I allowed it to continue. So, whenever I found that the cassette tape was playing, I needed to stop and 'change the tape'. I needed to consciously choose to change the inner narrative. So, instead of judging – bless. Instead of self-pity – pray.

It was such a helpful picture, that a few months later, I even used it in a talk where I recorded lots of negative statements, such as, 'You are no good', 'You will never get over this', 'You have no future', 'No one likes you', and more. As I started the talk, saying lots of encouraging things about who we are in Christ, the tape was played at the same time and same volume as me speaking. People looked confused and some even tried to get my attention to stop, pointing out that something was wrong. The point was easy to make. It is difficult to hear the truth when we are listening to a destructive tape at the same time. For younger readers, a cassette tape is what we had before the age of CDs and, for even younger readers, CDs are what we had before digital downloads and streaming!

Minutes after that point on Cromwell Avenue, I had to stop again and 'change the tape'. I found that it took months of recognising where my mind had drifted to and then 'changing the tape' and, choosing in the strength that God gives, to think differently – to listen to a different inner narrative.

I knew that we could not afford to allow unforgiveness, bitterness and self-pity into the foundations of this young church. If we did, it would be a fatal flaw in the building.

I think it is Dr Martyn Lloyd-Jones, in his book *Spiritual Depression*, who helps us to see that lots of our problems occur because we listen to ourselves, rather than talk to ourselves. If the inner narrative in our life is telling us things that do not line up with the Good News, then we need to change the narrative. Change the tape of unbelief and mistrust and choose to believe the Good News that our Saviour brings.

We recently spent some time with some new friends in the Bay area of California, who are leaders in the Soma network of Churches. They say that discipleship is the process of grace in our lives, where we move from unbelief about the Gospel, to faith in the Gospel in every area of our lives – so helpful!

As part of this inner journey, I had to see my own faults but also not to blame myself for things that I had not done. I had to realise that forgiveness is not saying that what happened is okay, but that even though we thought it was wrong, I have been forgiven so much and now I get to forgive.

I realised again that forgiveness is a process and that I needed to keep choosing to forgive and choosing not to be self-righteous or self-pitying. This wasn't easy and, to be honest, some days were better than others. I am so grateful that God sees our heart and patiently perseveres with us, so that we can see breakthrough.

I am so thankful that the people who I had the issues with, have met with me and we have talked and have come to a place of reconciliation.

Who is God asking you to be as a people?

This is such a key question. It is not what the latest idea to be popular on the church scene or the new best-selling book that gets to define who we are – these things can be helpful, but it is God who ultimately gets to define who we are.

Be to Do

Know who you are and then discover what you should do. We knew that we were to be a certain type of people. We were to live lives as individuals and as a people that reflected the three key priorities that we saw in the life of Jesus,

- Up – we are to have a growing/deepening love relationship with God.
- In – we were to live with a feel of extended family and
- Out – we were to share the Good News about Jesus in word and deed with those around us, so that they could have the opportunity to follow Him too.

Our values helped to underpin this, and the structure of the church was not to give life but simply to support the life that God gives.

One of our observations is that, if you plant a church, sooner or later (usually sooner), people who are Christians will start to arrive. Some are sent by God and others come because they hope that you will be the church that they wish there was in the town or city; one that reflects their own preferences, tastes and usually 'hero preacher'.

When the church is small and starting, it is tempting to just go for numbers. It is easy to feel the pressure to adapt what you are doing just to keep the Christians who have arrived, with their list of requirements and preferences. They never quite state it as a bluntly as that.

So, in our early years and still today, we have to stand for who God has asked us to be. We have lost people over the years, and in those early days, because we would not be less missional, or because we believe in leadership, or because we don't have the particular style that the Christians are shopping for, or because was ask people to be involved and serve, because we believe that's what Jesus models for us. It is painful and difficult when people choose not to journey with us, but it is vital that we hold true to who God is asking us to be and to doing what He has invited us to do.

I must also say, for balance sake, that sadly we have also lost some people over the years because we have made mistakes. We have, on occasions, had low control and low accountability instead of high accountability and low control. This has proved to be painful because, when there is low accountability in a group, usually the person with the strongest personality takes control.

When we realised this, we had to observe and reflect on what had happened on those occasions. Then, as a leadership team, we have discussed what we feel God is teaching us by our mistakes. Then we plan what we should do, put some accountability in place and take action. We have changed our minds and changed our actions to line up again with who God is asking us to be and to do what He is inviting us to do.

On one occasion, in the early years of King's, we had to have a conversation with a couple who were lovely people but wanted us to be a different church to the one we believed God was asking us to be. I had to point out that we were only just getting started as a church and that the things they saw in us, about evangelism, leadership and other things, were true. If they didn't like this stuff now, they would like what we were going to be doing in a year's time even less. So, if they could not go with this, the best thing to do was to part as friends and for them to find another church, in which they would be happier. Communicating this was so hard because we didn't want to lose them, but we knew that we had to be who God was asking us to be – even if that meant slower growth. The mustard seed starts small and gradually grows – the Kingdom of God tends to be like that.

During the first five or six years of King's, we saw steady numerical growth. We would have clear steps to the outworking of our vision. We believe it is important that we have a vision, and a strategy by which that vision is achieved. We have always aimed to take our leaders with us on this vision, knowing that they are the key influencers of those they lead. So, how this would work out in practice is that Jacky and I would typically talk to our core leadership team about what we believe the next phase of the vision is. This would usually include a strategic component of how we could see this happen. The team would then have input into this and there would be ongoing prayer and discussion at this level of leadership for some months. Then, we would share this with those on the staff team for their input, questions and observations.

Next, those who lead Missional Communities would be brought into our confidence and they would be asked to give their input and comments on what they had heard. After this, other leaders would be brought into the loop. Again, they would be given opportunity to give their observations, input, questions and suggestions. All the time, we are aiming to fine tune what we believe God is asking us to do and how we are to do it. We want to set the direction and then, together, discover how this could look. I think it was Paul Scanlon, the former Senior Pastor of Life Church, Bradford, who said that when we lead, it is like saying we are building a car. What the colour, the horse-power, the interior design, amongst other things should be are all to be decided and discovered together, but we are not building an aeroplane. The perimeters of the vision are set by the core leadership team and then the leaders work on what this could look like.

Only when all of the leaders have had some time to hear and digest the vision, do we share it with the whole church. This is a lengthy process that takes months. We believe that this is a worthwhile investment of time as, by the time the whole church hears the next phase of the vision, those in leadership at least know it and most of them have had months to think and pray about it.

Von Moltke, the nineteenth century military commander, said, 'No battle plan survives first encounter with the enemy.' We don't know what we don't know until we begin to implement a plan. Having this in mind helps us to deal with the fact that we will have to make some adjustments and apply some 'on the ground learning' as we go about implementing the vision.

The introduction of our 'Leaders Weekends', for Missional Community Leaders and their teams, have proved to be very helpful in each Missional Community discovering how their vision fits within the larger overarching vision of the church. But more of that later.

Over those first five or six years, we had set goals for cell multiplication and communicated these goals and, on the whole, seen them achieved. The church was steadily growing in number and new cells were opening, though we did notice something of the pain of cell multiplication. People enjoyed being in their cell and meeting the new people that were added, but when we reached around twelve people we wanted them to multiply into two cells. Some people found this quite hard, as they had invested deeply into the relationships within their cell and when the time came to multiply, they felt that those relationships were just not the same.

Along with cell growth, came growth at the celebration. The school hall, that seemed so big to begin with, was beginning to feel more and more cramped. There was limited space for children's and youth work. We also noticed that, when the room reached a point of being full attendance, we seemed to reach a plateau and even a dip in numbers. People had not left, but they realised that, if you did not get to the Sunday celebration early or on time, it would be difficult to get a seat and so would miss some weeks. Being full on Sunday mornings was a nice problem to have, but it was still a problem that needed to be addressed.

Barrow Hall Theatre

We had been trying on and off for some time to rent a local high school theatre, in the building next to the primary school. We managed to get a meeting with the head teacher of the high school and he agreed to rent the theatre to us, along with some class rooms for youth and children's work if the school governors agreed – which thankfully they did.

So, our Sunday celebration was on the move again. I can remember the final Sunday in the primary school. The room was reasonably full, but we were moving to a hall that I would estimate had a seating capacity around three times greater than the room we were currently in, and thc financial implications were far greater too. There was a moment in that last celebration in the primary school when I thought, '*Oh no, what have we done? We are going to feel lost in that big theatre.*' Faith is not pretending that the challenges are not there it is being aware of the challenges and choosing to trust God anyway. We set off in faith.

The first Sunday in Barrow Hall Theatre felt like one of those landmark days for us. At one point in the service, we asked everyone who was there at the first meeting of King's Church in our living room to stand, then those who had joined us whilst we were meeting in our home were invited to stand. Next, those who had joined during the period that our celebration was in Whittle Hall Community Centre. Those who had joined through cells or celebrations whilst we were gathering in Barrow Hall Primary School were then invited to stand – this was by far the biggest group. Then, finally, those who were visiting us that morning were asked to stand with us. There was a massive round of applause to God as we saw evidence of His work amongst us so far. The band then led us in the song *'I'll stand with arms high and heart abandoned to the one who gave it all. I'll stand my heart Lord to you surrendered – all I am is yours.'*

A new chapter in the journey had begun, as we surrendered again to our Father and our King.

There was a sense amongst us that the next phase would be different. We needed some changes and developments to happen if we were going to see more breakthrough and if we were going to progress in being disciples who make disciples.

Little did I know that a meeting with a friend of a friend in Starbucks was going to be so significant for us.

Chapter 7

Seeds of the Future

I first met Steve Biltawi when he was the Director of Warrington Youth for Christ. We met because he had made a decision that had infuriated me. So, in the spirit of Matthew 18, we agreed to meet to sort things out. I was part way through what felt like an argument with Steve, when it dawned on me that I really liked this guy, in fact I thought we could be friends!

We have become good friends! We began to meet each Friday morning for at least an hour to walk and pray together. Steve started some 'huddles' for youth workers and church leaders in the town, once a month, and I went along and met some amazing people, such as Ian Moore and Dan Curtis who were both later to become members of the core leadership team at King's.

Steve is a real person of faith and, in 2007, he stepped down as Director of Warrington YFC to go to Sheffield with his family to join Paul and Ellie Maconochie's family, and another family, living in community for some months. Paul was then the leader of St Thomas Philadelphia Church. Steve was going to be immersed in their culture and to learn about how to make disciples using the vehicle of Missional Community, shared life and celebration. Following his time there, he and his family were going to return to Warrington to plant a church linked to St Thomas Philadelphia. This was the early stages of *'Covenant and Kingdom Network'*, which became *Kairos Connexion* – an interdenominational movement of churches seeking to make disciples of Jesus.

When Steve and Ruth returned to Warrington, we resumed our weekly meeting to walk and pray together as well as meeting in Starbucks to talk about what God was doing with us and those that we were seeking to disciple. I was inspired and encouraged by Steve's stories of pioneer mission with young adults, as he sought to find 'People of Peace'.

Paul would, on occasions, come over to Warrington to be with Steve to encourage and disciple him in what he and Ruth were doing. One day, Steve had arranged to meet Paul in Starbucks but couldn't get there. He called me and explained that Paul would be sat in Starbucks in Warrington town centre alone for an hour. Could Jacky and I go to sit with him until Steve could get there? I happily agreed.

This was to be one of the most significant meetings in the development of King's Church. As Paul talked with us, we could see the mixture of wisdom, gentleness, focus and godliness that had grown in Paul. He told us about the church in Sheffield and the journey they had been on in missional discipleship, the challenges they had faced and the breakthroughs they were seeing.

We had met Paul before, when he attended a meeting with some church leaders from Warrington who wanted to meet with Steve prior to his planting of the church. (As things developed, Steve and Ruth and their children later joined King's and are now valued members of the team.)

What we found with Paul was that he was giving language to things that we had been longing to see and do since planting King's. We had already read Mike Breen's book *Passionate*

Church and had really connected with the tool of Life Shapes, which helped to teach some of the Biblical principles of disciple making.

As we talked with Paul, Jacky and I could see that we had reached something of a limit in the way that we were doing things and there were some components in our structure and way of operating that needed to develop. Paul said that he believed our meeting was a 'God thing' and he invited us to be a part of the first Learning Community that they were running. They had already met once, but we could join and connect with the process. This is what we did. In fact we did the first and then the second learning community, a process that took around four years, as we wanted to really take our time to learn how to implement what we were discovering about what our next season could look like.

Learning Community

We could not find St Thomas Philadelphia. We drove round and round, Jacky, myself and Julia, one of our core leadership team members, getting more and more frustrated. We eventually arrived, a little late and flustered. The team there were so gracious and welcoming.

The Learning Community emersion would last for three days and there were four of them over a two-year period. On day one, we explore 'What is?' We think about where our Battles, Breakthroughs, Failures and Frustrations are. There is teaching by practitioners and lots of time to work with your team, as well as to feed back to other teams.

Day two's focus is on 'What could be?' – time for blue sky thinking. A good friend of mine, Phil Potter, was doing the teaching on day two. He told the story of St Marks Haydock and the journey that they had been on during his many years there. He told us about the research that Edwin Hall had done, on how people interact with one another in four spaces.

We have worked with this for some years now and our current outworking of it looks like this:

The intimate space of just a few people like Jesus, Peter, James and John – maybe like what we would now call a Missional Household or perhaps a Huddle.

The personal space like Jesus and the twelve disciples – something like a Missional Community.

The social space like Jesus and the seventy-two – a Base.

The public space like Jesus and the crowds – Celebration.

The day also involves time to think and dream as a team, as well as hearing from others on the Learning Community.

Day three is 'What will be?' Again, there is some teaching and input, but lots of time to think, pray and plan about the goals for your church for the next two years and then more specific steps to take in the next six months. We would take these plans back to our Leadership Team to discuss and implement them, in line with our ongoing vision, as described in an earlier chapter.

By the start of day two I thought that I had made a big mistake in joining this process and wanted to go home! It was during coffee, before the day began, that Paul must have seen how I was looking. He asked me how it was going and I said that I wanted to go home! He told me that he had felt the same on his first Learning Community and encouraged me to keep on – I am so glad that we did.

Hearing Phil Potter's story again was so encouraging and was a reconnection with an old friend, which has proved to be an immense blessing to us. As Phil spoke, something was happening in Julia and she later told us, through tears, that now she really got what we had been saying about the next phase of the journey for King's.

At this stage of our travel through time, we had two of the four spaces operating in King's: the personal space (cells) and the public space (celebration). We did have clusters, which were small groups of cells. The cell leaders would meet with a cluster leader and, occasionally, the cells would get together to do mission or have fellowship but this was not a Missional Community.

Over time, we became convinced that, as followers of Jesus, we are to follow His words, His works and His ways. The way that Jesus made disciples seemed to involve interaction in these four spaces and the level of time, input and intimacy seemed to go up, as the size of the space went down. We would have to discover what the implications of all of this were, for us, as we moved into this new season.

Following and Leading

Mike Breen very helpfully talks about disciples as being sheep from the front and shepherds from the back. We get to be both leaders and followers. We may be leading thousands, or we may just be leading one or two people, but being a disciple of Jesus involves making disciples of Jesus. We also get to follow. We have people in our lives who help us to increasingly be and do what Jesus is inviting us to be and to do.

It seems to me that a big temptation, for us, is to read the latest book or attend the latest conference to become inspired by the information that we have gained and then to rush to try to innovate and implement these new insights in our own context. However, the process of discipleship seems quite different to this.

In the Greco Roman *oikos* or household, there would be three stages of development. In the early years, information would be passed on by a teacher. Then, around the age of thirteen, there would be a season where the young person would spend time with the parent in the family business. This was a season of imitation. The young person would learn by observing and involvement. After these two seasons of life, then the person was free to innovate.

We learned that the three phases of 'Information', 'Imitation' and 'Innovation' are so important in the process of being a disciple who makes disciples.

Our season in the learning community, and beyond, gave us some very helpful information and also provided a context where we could imitate – we could learn from the experience of others. We would also be free to innovate – to discover what being a Family on Mission together should look like for us at King's Church.

One of the words that can be used to translate the word 'disciple', is 'learner'. I have often felt as a leader, a follower of Jesus, a husband and a dad, that I should be wearing 'L-plates'. I am a learner and there is so much to learn. As parents, we are adjusting how we bring our children up at each stage of their development. We would be very unwise to treat our young adult children as if they were still in pre-school. As our children get older, it is a constant learning process for us as parents. We get to move from being in a 'directive leader' role, to the role of a 'coach'. As our children became adults, we realised the immense value of regular focused prayer for them.

I remember having a conversation with both of our children individually to explain that I had never been the parent of adults before, but here is how I was thinking of doing it: I would continue to pray for them each day. I would aim to remember that I now had more of a coaching role. I would like permission to give my opinion on the choices and key issues in their lives, but I would seek to respect that they are adults who love and follow Jesus and so would seek to respect the choices that they make. I continue to learn how to be a dad.

We also continue to learn how to be a disciple and a leader. Being a learner means that we are willing to allow others to have access and input into our lives. We are willing to humble ourselves and remember that we do not have all of the answers and we are not all wise. God wants to lift us up, but He wants to do the lifting. If we lift ourselves up, He will humble us. If we humble ourselves, He will lift us up.

Clusters – 'isn't that a breakfast cereal?'

As previously stated, we had Clusters at King's, but they were groups of Cells that did not operate as a midsize group. There were Cluster leaders who gave leadership and support to Cell leaders. They would occasionally do things together as a group of Cells or as a Cluster, but this could not really be seen as shared life. There were those who talked about Clusters as people with a shared missional vision, operating as a midsize group. That is not how we used the word, but we liked what they were talking about and were ready go on a journey.

So, we began to redefine what we meant by Clusters. With the benefit of hindsight, I would say that we made a few mistakes on the way. For example, perhaps we would have been wiser to change the name to start with, from 'Clusters' to 'Missional Communities' – a change that we made a few years later. Also, we tried to encourage the Clusters that did exist to start to operate as if they were a midsize group, but they mostly did not have a common missional vision.

Perhaps the best outcome of this kind of process, is one that Neil Atherton (one of our Cluster leaders) oversaw. Over a couple of years, he helped the Cells in his Cluster to discover their own missional vision and then to set off on the journey of becoming Missional Communities.

As we set about doing the groundwork of moving from just Cell and Celebration, to adding Missional Community and Huddle into our disciple making at King's, we needed to make space for our pioneers and early adopters.

We were given some very wise advice by Anne Maclaurin, a leader at St Thomas Philadelphia at the time, that a good way forward was to pioneer a couple of new Missional Communities and to view them as experiments. That is what we did. We started a couple of 'experiments'. Using that phrase gave us permission to try things without pressure.

One of our Cell groups at the time was growing quite quickly. Their focus was young adults aged 18-30. They had heard some of what we had been saying about making disciples and missional vision and Clusters. They had a new vision developing.

They noticed that quite a lot of them had musical skills and abilities and, at the time, there was a TV show about choirs that was quite popular. They wondered what would happen if they used their skills and passion for music to start a choir, but to have a Cluster at the heart of it.

As they talked to us about this and discussed it with the Cell members, it became clear that this could be one of our 'experiments'. Those who wanted to be a part of the new pioneer Cluster would remain together and set out on this process. Those who did not want to be a part of this experiment would be helped and encouraged to find other Cells to belong to. They began to pray and plan and soon they had a venue and were making people aware that King's Community Choir would be starting.

On the first evening, they wondered if anyone would show up, but as they looked out onto the car park of the school they had hired, they could see cars starting to arrive and new people coming. From the very start, they were clear that the people leading the choir are all followers of Jesus from King's Church and that they would pray and offer prayer at choir practice. They explained that there would be a time, after practice, when people would gather – all were welcome, either in a pub or in homes, and that there would be discussion around the Bible, prayer and other faith related things.

A few things surprised us as we saw the choir in its early stages. Those leading it told us that they had gone from leading an 18-30s Cell to an 18-80s choir! The age range was quite wide with more mature people making up the numbers.

Also, they saw the impact of simply being open about the good news without forcing it on people. One lady came to one of the leaders within the first few months to say how much being a part of this community was impacting her life. She had, in recent years, suffered the loss of her husband and had taken to drinking a bottle of wine each night to help her to cope. She told Rachel that now she was only drinking a bottle of wine per week. The impact of being a part of a community, with Christ at the core, was beginning to show.

Over the coming years, the choir grew to around 100 people with many exploring faith and becoming followers of Jesus.

A second experiment that we ran at this time was reaching out to families whose children were involved in sports on Sunday mornings. In the core team were some families who themselves were in this position, and others who simply wanted to serve and help to reach out.

We would simply gather on Sunday afternoon for food and some family games or activities. These were followed by a short talk for the whole family. We did see some people come along, and good conversations took place as parents were at matches watching their children on the Sunday morning. At this time, we also took out a season long advertisement at the town's rugby league stadium which had the name and website of King's Church on it, and the phrase 'No Perfect People Allowed'. As a number of the families not only played sport but also went along to the rugby league matches, this also proved to be a helpful conversation starter for our new 'experiment'.

We did have some good contacts and interesting times. At one point, we even held a Bible study in the bar at one of the local amateur rugby clubs. However, what we found was that many of our ideas to serve and bless some of the teams were not received and, after some time, we closed the experiment down. Some lives had been impacted by the good news about Jesus and we had learned some very important lessons – not least the importance of having a Person of Peace in the people group that you are seeking to reach with the good news – more of that later.

Seeds and Dreams

With experiments in place and teaching on missional discipleship being given, we reached a point when we believed it was time to communicate that people had permission to try things. We would set the parameters of High Accountability and Low Control. We wanted people to ask what dream has God placed in their hearts? Who were the people that they wanted to serve and reach? Who did their heart break for?

It was one of our vision days and we bought thousands of sunflower seeds and put them in a large container. We realised that people needed to know that they have permission to follow what God was asking them to do. We longed to release the church into the mission. We are all missionaries and so we wanted people to live a lifestyle of being missionary disciples. We simply wanted people to know, and be confident, that this was one of the things that we get to do as followers of Jesus. We were in no way wanting to put people under pressure and launch a guilt trip, but we believe that God has put things, seeds, into the hearts of all of His people and we get to let them grow.

At the end of the talk, people were invited to come and take as many seeds as they would like and to go home and plant them. As they did this, we highlighted that we all get to know that God has placed dreams in our own hearts, which He wanted to see grow.

People were asked to think and pray about the people group that they would like to reach – it could be a neighbourhood or a network. Then, we asked them to come and talk to us about the dream that they had. If they could get about ten people to join them on this adventure, we would train them to lead a Missional Community (still called Clusters at this point) and would connect them with leaders for accountability, ongoing training and support.

We did not tell people who to reach or which missional vision to have. We simply set a large enough missional vision for their visions to sit in. We asked them what God was asking them to do (Low Control), and we asked them if they were doing what God had asked them to do (High Accountability).

It is encouraging to see what happens when we do this. It is when we get to see the amazing variety and creativity that is present amongst God's people. Permission seems to be a key. As leaders, it is easy to assume that the people we are leading feel like they have permission to follow their God given vision. However, all kinds of experiences in life can communicate the opposite. Maybe in a person's upbringing, they have felt shut down or restricted. This could have been in a workplace or even a church.

When we set clear parameters and a healthy culture, then we create an environment where God-given creativity can be released and can really flourish. Helping people to understand the culture, and to know where the boundaries are, is so important.

Pioneers and Developers

Clampitt and DeKoch, in their very helpful book, *Transforming Leaders Into Progress Makers*, talk about how different types of leaders, when working together, form platforms on which progress can take place.

At this stage on our journey, as a people, we began to explore the role and impact of different types of leaders and people. Some people are pioneers and they love to try the new thing; they love to explore and discover things by setting off and having a go. There are other people who like to see gradual ongoing progress; they like to see things work well and come to a place of maturity. Clearly, we need both kinds of leaders in order to see any new venture flourish.

Pioneers and developers seem to both attract and repel one another. In fact, in a marriage, both often are present. Initially, we see in the other person, qualities that we don't have and we find them attractive. However, over time, if we are not careful, the very things that drew us together can begin to pull us apart. We are wise to recognise and remember that both pioneers and developers are needed. Then, we learn to be thankful for the different contribution that each partner brings to a church, a missional community, missional household, workplace, family and marriage.

If we are not wise, the pioneers can feel frustrated and held back. When they feel this way, they can try to move things forward by hitting the accelerator, as it were. The developers, at this point can feel that they are not being heard and that things are moving too quickly, and so they hit the brake! Two people who are on the same team, in the same marriage even, who love and care for each other, pulling in opposite directions. If this continues, a serious strain can happen in the relationship or team and, if not addressed, the relationship will fracture and break in two.

The fact is that this can happen in marriages, in missional communities, in churches – in fact in any group of people. How often have we heard the sad news of a church split because one group wants to take hold of 'the new thing' and others in the church are less than convinced and so dig their heels in?

The truth is that pioneers and developers need each other. Pioneers keep us moving. They break new ground and help to take us into the future that God has for us. Developers help to secure this. They put substance, systems and structures in place, so that we can secure the ground taken and build on it. Pioneers and developers, together, do build platforms on which progress can take place.

Generally speaking, they each contribute something to the process of building the future, so a pioneer generally will bring a measure of flexibility and a developer generally speaking a measure of focus – we need both.

In fact, we see both of these characteristics in God Himself. God reveals Himself to us as both a *'Rock'* (Deuteronomy 32:4) and as *'Living Water'* (John 7:38-39). This gives us the picture of being both solid and flexible. As leaders, we need to be sure about what are the non-negotiables and where we can be flexible. We are to take the ancient truths of the Christian faith and present them in a way that people, in the neighbourhoods and networks of 21st century Britain, can understand and follow. These are skills that we continually seek to grow and develop in. Wise disciples of Jesus get to be both **Focused and Flexible.**

Focus: What are the right things that we need to keep doing? For us at King's, these would be things like:

- Purpose – Up In Out;
- Values – A B C D E;
- High Accountability/ Low Control;

- Following the words, works, wounds and ways of Jesus in making disciples.

Flexibility: There are seeds that God has put in each of our hearts – people groups, networks, neighbourhoods and needs. What has God put in you, that is unique to you, that you could be or do for Him? What will it take to move from where you are now as a disciple of Jesus and as a leader, to where you could be? You see, it is easy to slip into feeling that life as it is, is life as it will be.

God invites us to a future with Him that frees us to be the people that we truly are. As we journey towards doing all that we dream that we could do, God works in us to help us to be all that we could be.

It is important that we, as leaders, understand this. It will help us in our development as disciples of Jesus, and it will help us to help the people that we lead to grow as disciples of Jesus.

Pioneers and Developers

Clampitt and DeKoch help us to see four challenges faced by Pioneers and Developers. When we recognise a problem, it is an opportunity to grow, if we will humble ourselves and engage with the problem seeking God's help and the wise counsel of others. So, here they are:

- The problem of the status quo – staying in the nest instead of learning to soar. This attitude shows up in statements like – *'We've never done it that way before'*. We are not advocating change for change's sake, but being willing to change – to progress. Growth always involves change.

- The problem of fear – Wynne Lewis was the former General Superintendent of the Elim Pentecostal Churches. Before holding that role, he led Kensington Temple, in London, as it experienced a massive season of growth from around 500 people to 5000. In one of the lectures that he gave to us as students in Elim Bible College, he said, *'There is always trouble at borders'.* Whenever we move from one season to another; whenever we pioneer something new, there will be trouble. Some of this is the natural fear of change, which some people have, that causes them to react in certain ways. In addition to this, we have an enemy who does not want us to advance and one of his main weapons is fear and intimidation. The Bible tells us that *'Perfect love drives out fear,'* 1 John 4:18. As we allow the love of God to compel us, we move forward into what He has for us.

The antidote to fear is not faith, it is love. The Apostle Paul wrote that it is Christ's love that compels us (2 Corinthians 5:14). As stated earlier in the book this is a wonderful picture. The particular Greek word for 'compel' is used only one other time in the New Testament. It is found in the story of the woman with the issue of blood. Jesus is on His way to the synagogue leader, Jairus' house, to heal his daughter. He is surrounded by a crowd and He stops and asks, *'Who touched me?'* We now know that the woman came forward and acknowledged that it was her, but imagine how the disciples felt when Jesus asked, *'Who touched me?'* The disciples replied, *'The people are crowding against you,'* (Mark 5:31). This is the idea of being carried by the crowd, hemmed in on all sides and pushed in one direction. It is the same word as is in 2 Corinthians 5:14 – 'to compel'. When we experience Christ's love, we are compelled to tell the Good News. His love surrounds us and moves us in the direction that He has for us. Being moved on by love, is a far better option than being stopped be fear.

- The problem of fatigue – some people treat continuous improvement and growth as a goal, not a mindset. If it

> is just a goal, then when it has happened, you can tick it off; but if it is a mindset, then we are doing this on an ongoing basis. If that is the case, then we need a rhythm of life that makes this sustainable. It seems to me that Jesus gives us this, in John 15, when He talked about the gardener, the vine and the branches. There are different seasons that require different responses, as we: Abide, Grow, Bear Fruit, Experience Pruning, Abide again and repeat. As we recognise the season and respond appropriately, this guards us against the fatigue that can halt our progress. However, when we recognise the seasons and lean into them, we find that they are essential for us, if we want to continue to bear the fruit that God has for us over the long haul.

We could arrange the four seasons of John 15 into two groups: 'Abide and Prune' seasons and 'Growth and Fruitful' season.

Abide and Pruning – in these seasons it is helpful to focus on *relationships*. In these seasons we often feel cut back, reduced and like we are in 'a valley'. The good news is that rivers often flow through valleys. When in these seasons, it is good to mostly engage in spiritual disciplines that come easiest to us. There can be a decrease in activity, so focus on relationships. Simply sow good things into your life and the lives of those around you. The seeds of the Kingdom have life in them and, at the right time, they will become visible.

Growth and Fruitful – there is an increase in *resources*, so there will be more energy, people, ideas, finances, opportunities etc. These can be seen as 'mountain top' seasons. Rivers don't tend to flow over the top of mountains, so we need to excavate to get to 'water' – dig a well. This can involve engaging in new or increased spiritual disciplines of fasting, prayer etc. The temptation in seasons of growth and fruitfulness is to think that we are somehow making it happen. The increased focus on spiritual disciplines in these seasons helps us to remember that we are relying on God. This is a season to be active in reaping, gathering and equipping the new disciples.

The 'Lifeshape' that helps us to remember about the rhythm of life is the semi-circle. Which season are you in at the moment? Is it time to abide and respond to pruning, to sow good seed as you weep, knowing that the seasons will move on and the harvest will come?

Is it time to be active in reaping and releasing resources? Can you see the fields ready for harvest all around you? Will you rejoice because *'the joy of the Lord is your strength'* and you will need His strength to do His work?

- The problem of not knowing when to say 'no' – there are lots of things that we could do, but we need to be focused and know what we should do. Do not be afraid to say no, even to good ideas, if you do not think that they will help to build the future that God has invited you into. Creativity within well-defined parameters leads to productivity. We can make ourselves very busy and take on lots of responsibilities, but the question is, 'are the things that we are giving our time and energy to contributing to the future that God has invited us into?' If not, they could be distractions or even worse they could be leading you in the opposite direction. Focus is your friend this will help you to know when to say yes and when to say no.

Chapter 8

Leading – Better Together

In Luke 5:4, Jesus says, *'Put out into deep water and let down the nets for a catch'*. Then in, verses 6-7 of the chapter, the story goes on to say,

> *When they had done so, they had caught such a large number of fish that their nets began to break, so they signaled for their partners and the other boats to come and help them and when they came and filled their boats so full, they began to sink.*

It would seem that Peter and Andrew, as brothers, were in the same *oikos*/extended family, and the family business of that *oikos* was fishing. Some in the family/*oikos* would be those who actually caught the fish, others may work on maintaining the boat or cleaning and repairing the nets, some may be involved in selling the fish at market and others in managing the money and cooking for the family. Everyone in the family had a part to play. It seems here that the *oikos* of Peter and Andrew, and the *oikos* of Zebedee – James and John, worked in partnership to handle the catch. I love what Jeff Vanderstelt says, in that they would move in time from seeing nets full of fish, to houses and meeting places full of people.

These verses were very important to us from the very early days at King's. Through these and the accounts in Chronicles of David's mighty men joining with him, we knew that it was going to be important to know how to disciple, identify, welcome and release leaders.

More like Joshua than Judges

Jacky spoke to the leaders at King's prophetically a few years ago and the picture that she used became one that stayed with us.

God was telling us that, as a people, we are to be more like the book of Joshua than the book of Judges in our view of how we lead. In the book of Judges, the tribes often seem scattered and people tended to do what was right in their own eyes. This led to a cycle of decline, calling out to God, a judge being raised up, deliverance, complacency, decline, repeat! However, in the book of Joshua there was clear leadership. The tribes worked together as well as taking responsibility for their own areas. They moved as a nation of tribes, taking possession of the land that God had promised to them. The kind of church that God is inviting us to be requires this kind of gathered and scattered approach to leadership.

It is important to us as leaders at King's Church that we bring a strong sense of us being a family on mission. We are a network of disciples who are working in covenant with one another to see God's Kingdom established in this area. So, we will partner together to see the church fulfil its purpose. We aim to cultivate a real sense of us being together as leaders in this venture.

> *'Five of you will chase a hundred, and a hundred of you will chase ten thousand...'*
>
> Leviticus 26:8 NIV

Simon Sinek, in his book *Leaders Eat Last*, talks about 'The Circle of Safety'. Using his experience in the US Marines, he explains how it is vital that the Marines are united together. If there is inner conflict, then they don't have the focus and energy to properly engage and defeat the enemy without.

He reminds us of *Aesop's Fable*,

> A lion used to prowl around a field in which four oxen used to dwell. Many a time he tried to attack them; but whenever he came near they turned their tails to one another, so that whichever way he approached them he was met by the horns of one of them.
>
> At last, however, they fell-a-quarrelling among themselves and each went off to pasture alone in a separate corner of the field. Then the lion attacked them one by one and soon made an end of all four.

1 Peter 5:8 says,

> *Be alert and of sober mind. Your enemy the devil prowls around looking for someone to devour.*

We need one another as disciples of Jesus and as leaders. We are members of the same family and we are given the same commission by Jesus, to be disciples who make disciples. It is therefore vital that we operate in unity and that we are increasingly one.

Our relationships and times together as leaders are very important to us. We believe that the whole is greater than the sum of the parts.

Leaders at King's meet on a regular basis and in a variety of ways. This is illustrated in our Leadership Menu…

Our Leadership Menu

Leaders Weekends – These take place twice a year and are a very important part in the life of a Missional Community/ Missional Household. They comprise of three elements,

1. 'What is?' – how is your Missional Community/ Missional Household at the moment?

2. 'What could be?' – a scenario is set of growth and progress and we discuss, in teams, how this might happen.

3. 'What will be?' – each Missional Community/ Missional Household sets goals, based on what they think God is saying to them, for the following six months. This then provides the basis for the *'What is?'* section next time and thus helps with on-going accountability.

Following the Leaders Weekend, we contact each Missional Community/Missional Household leader to see if they have what they need to implement the plans that they have made. In the season between Leaders Weekends, the leaders are in fortnightly huddles where they can share how the plans are progressing. It is the progress on these plans that forms the basis for the 'What is?' section of the Leaders Weekend. This is one simple way of implementing High Accountability and Low Control with the teams who are leading the Missional Communities.

Huddle – Each Missional Community/Missional Household leader is in a Huddle led by one of the Leadership Team. The Missional Community Leader hosts a Huddle for their team. Huddles can be seen as the ligaments that help to hold the structure of King's together.

Mentoring – Discipleship involves 'Information', 'Imitation' and 'Innovation'. Where necessary, we can link a leader with another leader for input.

Base Team Meetings – A Base is where two or more Missional Communities or Missional Households come together, once a month initially for some months, and then twice a month on Sundays, to plant an expression of King's in an area. The aim is to grow to about 70-80 people and then to plant another. These Bases will orbit into the central Celebration on the weeks that they are not gathering in their area. They have a different feel to the central Celebration and to a Missional Community. The leaders gather each month to plan and to pray.

Vision Events – These are our leaders' meetings where we all gather together. These are times to sharpen our focus on our overall vision, receive input from guest speakers and enjoy social time together. We have often invited a guest speaker simply to come and spend time with our leaders rather than the whole church to give input or to inspire them. We recognise how much time, resource, prayer and energy our leaders expend, and we want to invest in them and ensure that they know that who they are, and what they do, is valued.

As a younger leader, I made lots of mistakes leading leaders. I would meet with them infrequently and announce things to them, rather than involving them in a process. The good news is that we get the opportunity to learn from our mistakes as leaders. So, we now try as much as possible to involve different leaders in the process of decision making. This then means that, as we operate as a group of leaders with different leaders having different levels of responsibility and different capacity, it is easier to see the vision implemented.

If we fail to do this, it can lead to vision fatigue; the unhealthy place, where vision is cast and set off on with great enthusiasm. However, the 'how to' strategy of the vision is not properly explored. So, when problems arrive, as they invariably do, there can be a tendency to give up on the vision and look for another one to re-engender the enthusiasm that has been lost. When this is done repeatedly, vision fatigue sets in and people become immunised against following the vision. Slow is fast! 'A mustard seed' that is given time to grow and develop, in the end, is much more effective than a big launch which is news to everyone but has no clear implementation process.

Having different leaders involved together in leading, helps to provide a healthy mix of pioneers and developers – vision casters, prophetic types and strategists who ensure that the texture and feel of the vision is communicated, as well as the concept. It seems that most people 'get the vision', when they experience something of it, get a taste of it, feel the texture of it. Leaders often think in concepts, but if we forget to let people experience how it will feel to live in the vision, we neglect a key communication component. Texture cannot be announced from a platform, but we are thankful to have people around us who help us to create contexts where people can have a taste of what we are inviting them into before it arrives.

As we involve different leaders with a variety of fivefold gifting, it helps us to ensure that problems are recognised and addressed, strategies developed, goals are set and visions are achieved. Those we are leading are motivated to continue to play their part in the vision as they see it bearing fruit.

Leading and learning

I started taking driving lessons when I was 17 years old. 'How hard can this be?' I thought. Lots of people drive cars and I must be more capable than at least some of them.

Following a number of lessons, I took my first driving test (I now know that all the best drivers pass on their third driving test). I knew that things were not going well when I was asked to do the three-point turn manoeuvre. As I was part way through the manoeuvre, I couldn't quite remember which way to turn the wheel, so took a guess and found myself back exactly where I began. 'I can do this,' I told the examiner. 'Drive on,' was his reply! Hitting the accelerator instead of the brake in my ‘emergency stop’ didn't help either! The examiner asked me to stop the car about half a mile from the driving test centre. He asked me some questions about the Highway Code and then informed me that I had not passed my driving test and that he had decided to walk back to the test centre. I was left alone, sat in the parked car, waiting for my driving instructor to arrive. I wondered how many other people had not even made it back to the driving test centre on their driving test?

I had made some progress. Initially I didn't know that I couldn't drive, but now I knew for sure that I could not drive! I had progressed from unconscious incompetence to the lofty heights of conscious incompetence. I guess this is the stage of leading a church into a new phase or vision, in which many leaders and churches give up and look for another vision.

However, if we don’t give up and have leaders around us who draw close and pastor us through this, we will come to a point of breakthrough. ‘Mirror, signal, manoeuvre’ was a three-word phrase that I became very familiar with. I needed to focus, to practice, to be in the moment and to be aware. I was becoming consciously competent and, at this point, I took my second driving test. Things were much better, but I wasn't quite there. However, with a little additional coaching, I had soon passed my driving test.

I am sure that I’m not the only person to have gone through that kind of experience when learning to drive. Now I can drive without having to think about it much. It comes naturally – unconsciously competent.

This is like the journey that disciples and leaders are invited to go on. We can see it in the journey that Jesus took His twelve disciples on over the three years of His public ministry. It seems that, to pass things on, we need to revert back to conscious competence – we need to remember how we do certain things and why, so that we can teach others.

As leaders travel through life together, it is important that we create relationships and spaces where these things can happen. Like Peter and Andrew, we need the people on the other boat – we can't do this alone. As Jack Johnson sang, we are 'Better Together'.

For more information on the Leadership Square that I have just described, please see the book *Building a Discipling Culture,* by Mike Breen.

Chapter 9

Have You Got Rhythm?

I love music, I enjoy listening to music around the house or in the car. I enjoy going to concerts to see bands. I am often moved as we sing to God in worship. I can even play a few chords on a guitar, but my big problem is that I struggle with rhythm.

There was a time in the 1980s/90s when, in certain Pentecostal and charismatic churches, it was popular to do a sort of dance during the more upbeat praise songs. It was a sort of simple hopping from one foot to the other, with arms either by your side or slightly raised – a kind of *'River Dance'* – maybe more of a stream to be honest. I must confess that I too would join in, but what I noticed, and often had pointed out to me, was that my attempt at dancing bore no resemblance to what the beat and rhythm of the song was doing. In fact, I was completely out of time with everyone else who was dancing! As they were going up, I somehow seemed to be coming down and when they were coming down, up I would go!

Even when clapping along to a song, if I don't watch someone else, I find that I am like the kid in *Sesame Street* in the 1970s – 'One of these kids is doing his own thing.' I clap my own off beat, out of time rhythm.

A healthy life has a healthy rhythm. Leaders know this and are aware of its importance. For Missional Communities to flourish, they each need to find their own rhythm. The leaders set this. We have found that it is best to think in terms of a month or a six-week academic half term. There will be times when the whole Missional Community are together, other times when they gather in smaller groups or meet for huddle. There will be occasions where the main focus is Up, In or Out. The organised and predictable patterns help people to connect and, from this, all kinds of organic connection for meals, outings, coffee etc. can spring.

Each Missional Community is free to set its own rhythm, one that works best for the people in that Missional Community and for the people that they are trying to reach and serve. So, there is not a 'Missional Community evening' at King's, but Missional Communities gather on various days and at all kinds of times. Attending one of the celebration gatherings on Sunday is also seen as a part of the rhythm of the Missional Community.

There are regular patterns of prayer, eating together, Bible study, mission, fasting, etc. that are bespoke to each Missional Community. Sometimes, they gather in homes or coffee shops, they rent community centres or school halls, they may meet in the pub or the park, they are flexible enough to find ways to really connect with each other and with the people that they are trying to reach and serve. The aim is that the gatherings, whether organised or organic, all contribute to reinforcing the culture of being a Family on Mission together – this is not simply a series of events…it is a lifestyle.

One of the most exciting seasons in the life of King's Church for me were those early days in St David's Drive thinking, praying, eating and planning with a group of friends about how we could impact people with the Good News about Jesus. When we release Missional Communities, we give them the opportunity to have the same kind of experience. They are a band of disciples on a mission to be and bring good news to each other and those who are not followers of Jesus.

Nuts and bolts of the time machine

We get to learn from the past, live in the present and live for the future. As we do this, there are certain things that help us to live as disciples who make disciples; some simple nuts and bolts of community and mission that help us to live here and now as citizens of the city to come. Here are some of them:

Prayer – Missional Communities and Missional Households provide us with a great opportunity to strategically saturate an area in prayer. You get to spend time praying for every household in the neighbourhood and, where possible, for the people who live there by name. One of our Missional Communities printed a map of all the streets in one area of Warrington and, over a number of weeks, prayer walked every one of them. One of our Mission Households has three families who live very close to each other. They prayer walk between one another's homes regularly each month and then take it in turns hosting something in their home, where they can invite neighbours in to get to know each other and find out more about Jesus. There are so many ways to raise the level of focused prayer.

One way is to prayer walk your area – the same streets – on a regular basis.

'One Life' is the name of the Missional Community that Jacky and I currently lead. One Sunday morning, we were out prayer walking and litter picking in our local area. We split up into smaller teams and planned to meet at the pub later for a full English breakfast. One team were litter picking around the pub when one of the managers came out and asked what they were doing. They explained that they were local Christians, that they love the area and wanted to bless and serve it. The manager asked how many of us were out doing that this morning, I think there were about fifteen of us. He then said that, as a thank you, he would like to invite us all back for a free full English breakfast when we were done. What a great idea!

It is important when prayer walking to lift up our eyes and see the harvest. Look at what is happening around us. Be observant and ask questions. When you meet people as you are prayer walking, here are some questions that you could ask,

- 'We are a local group of Christians wanting to serve and pray for our area. What do you think we should be praying for?' It is so helpful to get the insights of people. They tell us what the felt needs are in a community
- 'Is there anything we could pray about for your family?'
- 'Is there anything we could pray about for you?'
- 'Would you like us to pray for you now or later?'

Our Missional Community were recently out prayer walking and, as we walked, we began to pray for people who live on the estate who once walked with Jesus but now had drifted from Him. We began to pray for people by name, listing them before God as we walked. We had gone out in two groups that evening and the group that I was with got back to our meeting point outside Sainsbury's supermarket first. As we were waiting for the other group to arrive, Jane, one of the people we had been praying for by name walked out of Sainsbury's, came over to us and said that she thought it was time she came back to church! I asked her to contact Jacky, who was still out prayer walking with the other group, to arrange to meet up to talk about this. By the time we were home, Jane had phoned Jacky, they met for coffee and Jane is now walking with Jesus and an active member of our Missional Community. God hears and answers prayer – sometimes slowly, sometimes really fast, but always at the right time.

People of Peace – as Missional Communities and Missional Households reach out to neighbourhoods and networks, we are prayerfully looking for the 'people of peace'. These are those who are open to the Gospel themselves and who may be door-openers to families or sections of the local community.

There is no doubt in our minds that people matter to God and He wants as many as possible to come into His family. Jesus talks about the Least, the Last and the Lost. So, He says,

- The Son of Man came to seek and save the *lost* – Luke 19:10
- Whatever we do for one of the *least,* we do for Jesus – Matthew 25:40
- The first will be last and the *last* will be first – Matthew 19:30.

Often, people in these groups feel somewhat broken and alone. They come into a relationship with Jesus and they are like the lonely being welcomed into a family. Whether they are aware of it or not, they really need connection with the family of God, as belonging will be a part of their journey. When one of the *least, last* and *lost* becomes a follower of Jesus, the family of God grows by addition. They are equally valuable to everyone else as all people matter to God.

However, in places like Luke 10:1-12, Jesus talks about 'People of Peace'. These people are often not alone – they are connected to a people group and can potentially open that people group up to the good news.

Have you ever noticed that sometimes you see something for the first time in Scripture and, when you see it once, you start to then recognise it all over the place? For me, the 'person of peace' teaching of Jesus is like that. Once I saw it, I then began to see it in how Jesus called His disciples, what He taught them to do, then the experience of the early church in Acts, not to mention in my own experience and in the experiences of others around me! It is everywhere!

There are people who, when they become a follower of Jesus, suddenly a group of others do too. So, in the Bible, an example would be people like the Philippian jailer. He and his household believe. Another example would be Lydia. She and her household believe. Often, when this happens, these people connect with the existing family of God and there is potential for a new expression or new Missional Community or Missional Household or new church to be planted. When a person of peace becomes a follower of Jesus, there is potential for the Kingdom of God to grow by multiplication.

Remember the least, the last and the lost are equally important to the person of peace, but it can be helpful to recognise who we are dealing with so that we know what that person needs and how best to help them to grow as a follower of Jesus.

Go with someone – in the original teaching on this, Jesus sends the twelve and the seventy-two out in twos. As we reach out into a neighbourhood or network, don't go alone. We need each other. It is not family *or* mission, but family *on* mission.

Say something – lead with the Gospel. That doesn't mean that you have to say everything to start with, but you need to say something. Jesus said to say that *'the Kingdom of God is near'*. So, something like, 'God is near to you. Would you like to know more about that?' This isn't a script, so think about how you could best express it as you. If they say yes, then tell them more. If they say no or not yet, that's okay. If they want to know, we want to tell them more. If they don't want to know, we don't want to force anything on them, but there must be a point at which they get to choose.

Heal something – Jesus said that when we are looking for people of peace, we get to heal the sick. So, if as you are looking for people of peace you notice that someone is unwell or has a need, then offer to pray for them. If there is no obvious illness or they don't tell you about one, then observe – what is 'sick' in this neighbourhood or network? What would it look like to bring healing to that? Then do something!

Eat something – we need one another. We are not the experts and we can learn from everyone. So, when we are looking for people of peace, we don't come in with pride and all of the answers, but with humility and a willingness to serve and to be served. As I am writing, we are in lockdown due to the Covid 19 pandemic. When the schools closed, we were concerned that the children who were receiving free school meals, may go hungry. With that in mind, we started to open our community centre and ask people to donate food and then took that food to families in need. This has become known as 'King's Table'. One lady in Grace Missional Community put a box on her drive and asked her neighbours if they wanted to contribute – they did. So, Jacky took up that idea and we, along with Paul and Rachel who lead YAK Missional Community and live next door to us, put a letter through the doors of all the homes on our street. We explained about 'King's Table' and asked if they would like to provide some food for families in need in our town. Before Jacky got back from delivering the letters, food started to arrive! When we allow people to serve and bless us, we humble ourselves and a connection is built.

Deal with something – Jesus did say that, as we live as a family of missionaries, there would on occasion be opposition. We see examples of this throughout the book of Acts. Perhaps this is one of the reasons why Jesus said that we are best not to go alone, as we are going to need each other to keep going.

Organised and organic – healthy families don't just interact for ninety minutes on a weekend, where one person does most of the talking, and then for ninety minutes on a Wednesday night sat in a circle – they share life. However, they do have certain points in their rhythm of life when everyone knows what is happening. It may be an evening meal around the table,

Match of the Day on Saturday night or visiting grandparents on Sunday afternoon – you get the picture.

In the life of a Missional Community or Missional Household, there is space for lots of organic, spontaneous connection (this is why it is important not to cram the church programme). There are also points at which there are regular organised things that people can gather around to 'keep the family healthy'. Things like, exploring the Bible together, praying together, doing mission together, fasting together and eating together.

There are three ways that the New Testament finishes the sentence, *'The Son of Man came...'*

- *'...not to be served but to serve and to give His life as a ransom for many.'* Mark 10:45
- *'...to seek and save the lost.' Luke 19:10*
- *'...eating and drinking.'* Luke7:34

Luke's gospel speaks of at least nine meals that Jesus ate with His disciples and others, and there are many more examples in the New Testament. I don't think that Luke and the other writers are just pointing out the humanity of Jesus and His need to eat – though of course there is that. Tim Chester, in his book *A Meal With Jesus,* says,

> This is why eating and drinking were so important in the mission of Jesus: they were a sign of his friendship with tax collectors and sinner...In the ministry of Jesus, meals were enacted grace, community and mission.

Jesus ate with other people a lot – and we get to too.

We have 21 meals each week. Who could you invite to share some, or one, of those meals with you?

Here are a couple of simple hints,

- Keep it simple so that you can show those in your Missional Community that they can do this too. So, don't go for the elaborate four course dinner. Jacket potatoes and chilli, bangers and mash, spaghetti bolognese and pizza are great. As you eat together regularly as a Missional Community or Missional Household, the meal becomes an open table and can be a seed of multiplication.

- Invite guests who are not followers of Jesus, so they get to *'taste and see that the Lord is good'* in the food and the atmosphere of extended family.
- After food, it is good to have a time of thanksgiving where everyone has the opportunity to say briefly something that they are thankful to God for, or something good that has happened in their week – this second question is particularly good if they are not a follower of Jesus and are not comfortable with thanking God. It can also be good to have some simple prayer, or to read something like the New Testament daily Moravian reading.
- Caesar Kalinowski suggests that if there are lots of guests, perhaps over the meal at various points ask everyone to respond to questions like: Where were you born? What is your favourite childhood memory? What is the worst job that you have had? There are many more! It is surprising where the conversation goes.

Tell and show Good News. Eugene Peterson says, in *The Message* version of John 1, that Jesus *'moved into the neighbourhood'*.

Jesus went with His disciples to a family event where He turned water into wine. The first miracle of Jesus happens not at the temple or in the synagogue, but at a family do.

We get to be with people in their context and bring good news in word and in deed. Miracles can happen in community. It seems to me that most of Jesus' miracles happened in the run of life and not in a meeting.

For some of us, this means to think about where we already are; our neighbourhood, workplace, school or office. What would be a good next step for you? How could you raise your head above the parapet and bring good news in that place?

Cross-blades is a Missional Community which reaches out to a local ice skating and ice hockey community. During games, at half time and after the match, they litter pick around the seats. One person from Cross-blades is responsible for the score board on match days. They provide a welcome goodie bag for the referee each week. These are ways to show simple acts of kindness and being good news, so that their words and deeds match up.

What does it mean for you to be a presence in your community? What could that look like? It will look different in each setting.

In one of the local communities where one of our Bases is centred, they have a summer fair. Some people from the Base got involved in the planning group. When the minutes from one of the meetings were emailed out, they were surprised to find that one of their responsibilities was the weather! They would pray for good weather for Saturday, July 6. If we are not in the community, there is not the opportunity for the miracle to be shown or seen. Presence opens up networks in your community to you quite easily if you will simply be there, commit to prayer and be consistent. As we show up, then relationships and networks will open up.

Do something that is good news in your community. Missional Communities have done things like forest trails, family canoe days, litter picks, walks, food collections for families in need and fish finger suppers to name a few. We look for what is broken and try to contribute to its healing.

The beauty of doing this in Missional Communities, Missional Household and Bases is that we get to be bespoke to the people group that we are seeking to reach and serve. We then get to stick with it as often breakthrough takes some time. Motivation is key. If it is not born out of love, it usually doesn't last too long.

In John 2, we read about Jesus and His disciples going to a wedding. A special but not unusual event. In that family and community context, Jesus performs the first of the signs through which He revealed His glory, and His disciples believed in Him.

The disciples discover who Jesus is through His presence at a wedding in the community, not at a synagogue or at the temple. John tells us that, as soon as they recognise Jesus' identity, they are ready to follow Him. As disciples of Jesus, we get to carry His presence into our world. We get to display the identity of Jesus in our community. In order to do this, we must be present with them, so that they get the chance to 'recognise' who Jesus is in us. We read of the Jerusalem church in early chapters of Acts doing just that. They built a community that looks like Jesus and then impacts a city.

Pathways to faith – These are the spiritual journeys that we invite people on. Clearly there is groundwork to do before people are ready to step onto a pathway of faith.

It's really helpful to have tools like Discovery Bible Studies, Alpha, Story Formed Way etc. that we can build into the rhythm of the life of a Missional Community or Missional Household. When Paul was travelling, he seemed to have a 'process' that he could use over a long, or short, time to help people to understand the message of the Gospel. Some people think that we have the major elements of that process set out for us in the book of Romans. This is a book that Paul wrote to a church that he had not yet visited, which lived in the city at the centre of the known world. He does not seem to address any major pastoral issues in the book, though in chapter 16 we discover that he already knows lots of the people in the various households/*oikos* in the church in Rome. He uses this book to set out the main themes of the gospel that he preaches.

In Thessalonica, Paul went into the synagogue and reasoned with them on three successive Sabbath days. He faced opposition and moved on to Berea where, yet again, a process takes place. Here Paul spoke regularly at the synagogue, but they 'daily' examined the scriptures and responded much better there. In Corinth, he integrated into the *oikos* of Priscilla and Aquila, working as a tentmaker. Every Sabbath, he reasoned with the Jews and Greeks at the synagogue. When they rejected him, he went next door (Acts 18:7) and the whole household responded. Paul stayed there a year and a half teaching the word of God. Paul seems to engage in process, not merely a series of one-off events. The process could be reduced to three weeks or extended to months, but there seems to be a body of teaching that Paul wants people to grasp to help them to begin and continue the journey of discipleship.

Paul seems to have a 'Pathway of Faith'. He would be flexible and open to change within that strategy. We get to think about how we use process, as we bring the message of the Gospel.

Paul was in a context that was pre-Christian. Here he would talk through with people what the Gospel means. We, in the west, live in a culture that is largely post Christian – and so in many ways not dissimilar to Paul. If we are to reach people and help them to grow as disciples, we would be wise to provide places where people can process their questions about faith and the word of God – a pathway to faith.

We would encourage you to find a process that is good for you, then do it. Fit it into the annual rhythm of the life of your Missional Community or Missional Household. Nic and Jenny Harding lead a Missional Household in Liverpool. They run Alpha in their home every autumn. One of the people in their

Missional Household challenged everyone to get ten refusals to invites to Alpha! It worked well and new people came.

It is an immense privilege to journey with people before they respond to Jesus and become His follower. This is part of the discipleship journey for us and for them. We are convinced that discipleship begins before someone makes the commitment to become a Christian.

Jan started coming to King's Community Centre after being invited by a neighbour who lives near the centre. Jan had gone to church when she was younger but wasn't a follower of Jesus. She was invited to Grace Missional Community, which meets in KCC, and was interested in joining a Discovery Bible Study. Jan really enjoyed the group and did the "homework" every week and gradually felt confident enough to share what she was learning.

After the Discovery Bible Study ended, Jan kept going to Grace Missional Community and after twelve months, she made a commitment to accept Jesus as her Lord and Saviour.

Here is her story,

> Since doing the Discovery Bible study with Grace Missional Community and reading the scriptures, I seem to have a deeper understanding of what they mean to me and what the Lord is saying to me. To have faith and serve Him by helping others and loving one another even when times are dark.
>
> He's always with me and I love to give thanks and praise Him for being in my life because of how He loves me. He died on the cross for me and I love the Lord deeply because He brings me peace and hope and joy in my life. And I thank you, Lord, for filling me with the Holy Spirit every day of my life. *Jan*

Romans 5:5 – *'The love of God has been poured out in our hearts by the Holy Spirit who was given to us.'*

One of the leaders of Grace Missional Community wrote,

> My experience of leading a Discovery Bible Study has been a very positive one. Our Missional Community has, so far, offered three Discovery Bible Studies; one in a home and two at King's Community Centre. Average numbers at each one has been between four and six guests and two people leading.
>
> We studied John's gospel and looked at well-known Bible stories, even to those who hadn't had much connection with church. Each session gave a different aspect to the stories, bringing them up to date and relevant to the individual. As we know, God's timing is perfect and, in some cases like Jan's, it took another year for her on her journey of faith to reach a decision. In another person's life, they made a commitment during the Discovery Bible Study.
>
> I would certainly recommend the Discovery Bible Study as a way of helping people to reach a decision in their lives to become a disciple of Jesus.

Disciple-maker's journey – we have the privilege of developing ways to help new followers of Jesus to become disciple-makers themselves. A useful tool for this is *The Disciple Maker's Journey* that Nic Harding developed:

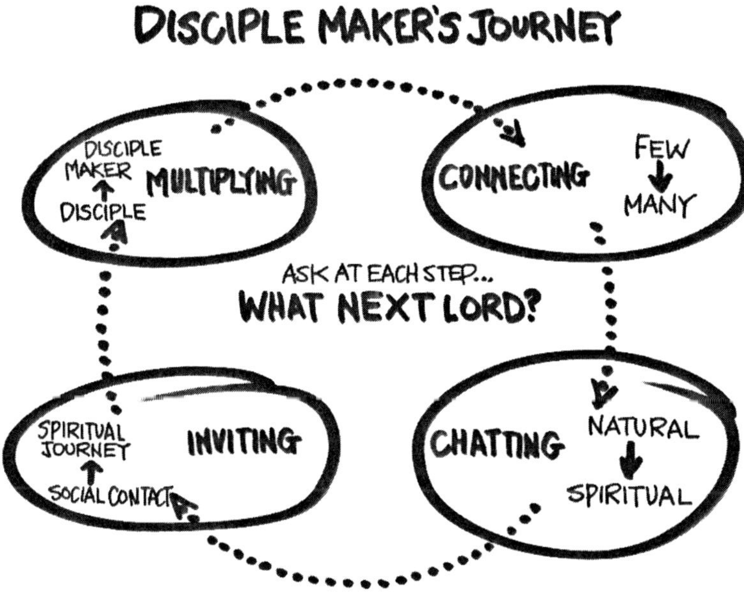

Connecting

We connect with people all the time wherever we are – at work, in our streets, at the school gates, in the gym etc. Why not be intentional with these connections? The truth is that we need to make dozens, if not hundreds, of connections if we are to find people of peace. The challenge, or if you like the journey within the journey, is to go from few to many connections. Too many of us think that the key to successfully winning people to Christ is to invest in a few relationships over many years and hope that they become open to Christ. Sadly, this doesn't often happen. Unless we have a way of figuring out who might be a person of peace, then we may have some lovely friendships, but never have the joy of leading anyone to Christ, and we will miss the many who are searching.

Once we have begun to suspect who the possible people of peace are, then we will start to invest more in the few. The simplest way to make a connection is to say 'hello'.

Chatting

This is not rocket science is it! But when we get into conversation, we are starting to pick up all sorts of signals, we need to listen. We are not treating people like a project – no one wants to be our project. It is because we love God and we love people that we want to be focused and attentive to the opportunity to help people to connect with the God who loves them. As we are chatting, we are asking ourselves and the Holy Spirit – 'Are they interested in the good news?' 'Are they listening to what we have to say?' 'Is there a connection between their story, our story and God's story?'

The challenge at this stage is moving from natural to spiritual conversation. For many of us, this is profoundly difficult, and we have made many faltering, awkward attempts to do this. There are many ways of introducing spiritual topics to the conversation, like talking about going to church, God answering your prayers, but best of all is sharing your faith story.

Learning to tell your story in a natural and non-cringey way is both an art and a skill. There are many hints on how to do this one, but what we recommend is to simply think about your story in three stages: Before, How and Now. These act like three pegs on which to hang your story. It is good to have both two and five minute versions, depending on the context. Because your story is your story, no one can argue with it. That's why it's so powerful. It's easy to bring our story in to pretty much any conversation. It is good to ask people lots about themselves. Be genuinely interested, but also know that, usually at some point, they will ask you something about your life. Somewhere along the line you can usually say something like, '…You know what…can I tell you my story?' If they say yes, then you have permission and don't need to feel bad about telling it. Once you have told your story, it's easy to see if they are 'leaning in'/ interested or not. If they are, then you can follow it up with questions about their experience of faith, God, or whatever spiritual topic seems appropriate.

Inviting

By now you are getting a good idea who your potential people of peace are, certainly enough of an idea to risk inviting them to something. Initially, the invitation is to create a relationship, so is likely to be to some kind of social contact in a neutral setting, such as a coffee shop or pub, or possibly to a meal that your Missional Community or Missional Household is hosting. It's important that the relationship of trust and friendship grows and allows more free and frequent spiritual conversations (as well as all the usual stuff of life). The challenge will be in taking the friend from social contact to spiritual journey. Most people don't come to Christ via a one-off event, though some do. For most, it's a process of questioning, toe dipping and taking small steps in the direction of personal faith. So, we need to create those stepping-stones to faith so we can help someone take those small steps that lead to a big life change.

Multiplying

It might at first seem strange to go straight from inviting to multiplying disciples. But I believe as soon as we start to engage with people of peace, we are entering a discipling relationship – they just don't know it yet. They are watching your life. They are learning about your priorities, your lifestyle, your relationships, the way you talk, the way you deal with frustration and anger and, above all, about your relationship with Jesus. You are discipling them. By the time they commit to the stepping-stones to faith, they are well on the way. They may not have crossed the line of salvation (though that is often difficult to define), but they are following and you are leading. So, by the time they do commit their lives to Christ, you need to be thinking about how they can be influencing their own peer group, family, neighbours and work colleagues etc.

The challenge is to help them grow from disciple to disciple-maker, and so enter the disciple-makers journey. At this stage of their Christian life, they will have so many family members and friends who don't know God and it's wonderful to see them having impact on them and leading them to Christ. They become a disciple-maker and you become a multiplier.

Chapter 10

We're Going to Need a Bigger Boat

One Christmas time, a few years ago, I was stood outside M&S store at the Gemini retail park in Warrington waiting for Jacky to come out – she is store Chaplain. The car park was crowded as were the roads leading in and out of the retail park. I remember being close to tears – and not at the thought of having to go Christmas shopping! I was overwhelmed as I saw all of the people. There seemed to be people everywhere. I wondered what I would say when I stand before Jesus if He asked me what I had done to give every man, woman, young person, boy and girl an opportunity to hear the Good News in a way that they could understand and respond to and, if they said yes to Jesus, how would we help them to live as His disciples?

In the famous words from the *Jaws* film, I realised – we were going to need a bigger boat!

Back in 2017, Warrington Borough Council estimated that the population of the town was 209,700 people. Recent estimates, which include some of the outlying areas of the town, could push that number as high as 220,000 people.

It seems obvious to me that trying to attract everyone to one church building or to one Christian ministry will never get the job done. But what if we released God's people as Missionary Disciples into their neighbourhoods, workplaces, networks and friendship groups etc? What if we partner as churches and Christian organisations so that we saturate the town and the surrounding areas with the Good News of the message of Jesus? How could we do this? How could we see the Good News about Jesus go viral in our town?

What if we planted an expression of church for every thousand people in our town and surrounding area? That does not necessarily mean loads of new church plants, though it could, but we could release people into neighbourhoods and networks to be missionary disciples, bringing the Good News of Jesus in a way that the people around them can understand and respond to. Then we could provide a space where those new followers of Jesus could grow as disciples.

What would be the essential ingredients in each of these expressions of church? They could be networks of people where we work out how to live the greatest commandments and the Great Commission. Living out a simple three dimensional life as a disciple of Jesus,

- God focused – loving and worshipping Him – *Up*
- Strong sense of family and fellowship – *In*
- Sharing the Good News with those who don't know Jesus and seeking to make new disciples – *Out*

Our aim is that, with our deeds and our words, we create the possibility for every man, woman, young person, girl and boy to hear about Jesus in a way that they can understand and respond to and then have a place where they could grow as His disciples.

Words and deeds are vital. Our friend, Gary Gibbs, tells the story of a Christian family moving onto a housing estate and deciding that they were going to reach their neighbourhood just with their actions. They would wait for people to ask them questions about their faith before they spoke. After some time, one of the neighbours said to them that they and some of the other people on the street had been talking about the Christian family. They said that they had noticed there was something different about them and had been discussing what it was. They were sure they had worked it out – 'we know what is different about you…you are vegetarians aren't you?' Our deeds alone won't get the job done. People will notice that there is something different about us, but they may never ask what it is, or they may just think that we are nice people. The Good News is best expressed in words and deeds.

The *One in a Thousand Vision* is by no means unique to us, nor did it originate with us, but it is something that we believe that God is inviting us to live towards. We are a long way from being in a place where this one in a thousand vision will be fulfilled, but it can be fulfilled and there are places in the western world that have seen things like this already happening. Our desire is not to copy them, but to be who God is inviting us to be, here and now.

Over recent times, we are excited by the fact that other churches in Warrington have also embraced this vision and, together, we are exploring how best to saturate our area with the Gospel of Jesus and disciple making communities.

We are at the early stages of this, but we are embarking on a journey of trust with each other so that we are confident that we are not trying to build our own empire, or promote ourselves or our own church. We are in a moment when we have started a new chapter together as Church Warrington. No one is foolish enough to think that it will be without its challenges, but if we can learn to be difficult to offend and quick to forgive them we stand a chance. We are learners together.

What did the Romans or the Celts ever do for us?

After the fall of the Roman Empire, Christianity began to decline in parts of the British Isles as invaders came from mainland Europe. The Celtic Christians, however, held fast and continued to reach people, building communities of followers of Jesus.

It was around that time that Pope Gregory I sent a missionary, called Augustine, to England with a small group of people. Their job was to set about re-evangelizing un-Christianized Anglo Saxon England. When they first landed, they found the test far more difficult than they had anticipated and retreated back to France. The Pope heard about this and was insistent that they go back to Britain. They did this and set off for London but only got as far as Canterbury, where they set about building a cathedral. It was the biggest building that people in the area had ever seen. Can you imagine what impact on the senses the services, held in that cathedral, would have on those early visitors? They would find themselves in a large and impressive room with stained glass windows and coloured light flooding in. Incense would be burning, filling the air with a rich, sweet smell and the haze of smoke. The sound of the music and singing would be amazing. They built this amazing celebration centre that reached some people, but it was never going to change the entire nation.

In 664AD, there was the Council of Whitby, where both the Roman and the Celtic missionaries met together. There is some debate about the significance of this council, but the lasting outcome was that the 'Minster System' came into being. The result seems to have been a combination of what both the Romans and the Celts had to bring. The Minster became a large centre for mission and discipleship in an area. Each Minster had an Abbot, linked to the word 'Abba' – 'Father', so there was a sense of extended family there. Orbiting in and out of the Minster, there would be a travelling bishop who would work from the Minster with smaller expressions of church in each community. These were all linked to the Minster. They would all gather at certain points in the year, but then went back to their local areas to live out their faith where they lived and worked.

This reminds us of the model of household and temple that we read about in Acts 2. When this happened, a missionary movement was birthed that impacted not just this nation, but the whole of Europe.

Why the history lesson? Because we see this in the Book of Acts, and we see it at key points in church history. That, when we as followers of Jesus take seriously God's invitation into radical community with other followers of Jesus, when we have a balanced outlook of Up, In and Out and when we gather in larger, mid-size and small gatherings to live out what it means to be a family on mission, then the world around us is changed. The question is not whether we should be 'Attractional' or 'Missional Church', but rather how do we blend the best of both to make disciples of Jesus in different sized spaces and in both formal and informal settings?

Wormholes – Keep Moving

Mike Breen, in his book *Building a Discipleship Culture*, talks about the importance of *Kairos Moments*. Those points in time when there is an opportunity to change our minds, change our actions and to see a greater in-breaking of the Kingdom of God. The quicker we recognise and respond appropriately to *kairos* moments, the faster the progress in our time travel. They act as 'wormholes' which, if engaged with, transport us forward more quickly.

The Council of Whitby acted as a *kairos* moment to move the purposes of God, in Britain and Europe, forward into a new phase. Jesus, moving from Nazareth and establishing a mission centre in Capernaum, was also one of those *kairos* moments, when the Kingdom of God moved forward more quickly because a new phase was entered.

If you play *Mario Kart*, it is like when you get a gold star and you move forward more quickly. So, it is vital that we are attentive to the possibility of the in-breaking of God's Kingdom on all kinds of levels and especially at those pivotal moments, when we are moved into a new phase of life as disciples of Jesus.

Oikos With The Doors Thrown Open

There is a lot of talk about the importance of small groups in disciple making. Small groups are better than no groups at all, but if they are just a midweek meeting added to a Sunday meeting, they will be limited in their effectiveness in the disciple making process. Shared life is the most effective way to live as, and make disciples. This involves the formal and informal settings of life. Small groups that are just about study and surface level friendship, and Sunday gatherings that are disconnected from the rest of life, will leave us disappointed in our goal of making disciples who make disciples. So, what did Jesus do? He is the greatest ever disciple maker, so what can we learn from Him?

The first five followers were Andrew, John, Simon, Philip and Nathaniel. In Luke 4, they attend synagogue with Jesus in what was to become His new hometown for a season, Capernaum. After the synagogue service, which Jesus regularly attended during His earthly ministry, He walked a couple of blocks to the *oikos*/household of Simon Peter.

Peter has a thriving fishing business and a nice home, but he is clearly looking for more from life. Peter is a Person of Peace to Jesus and, as such, he welcomes Jesus into his home. Jesus heals Peter's mother-in-law and He shares a meal with them – all things that He would later teach His disciples to do with People of Peace.

In this context of Peter's *oikos*/household, Jesus is about to redefine *oikos*. At the time, the *oikos* was primarily a place of provision and protection – a place of shared resources and shared living. Each nuclear family or couple had a room, or an 'Insular', that had a door facing into the shared courtyard. There would also be a large room in the household, which was a social place and a space to eat together as an extended family. There were no outward facing windows and the door to the courtyard, and into the *oikos,* was closed at sundown for protection.

In the account of the story in Mark 1, we are told in verse 33 that, as the sun was setting, Jesus kept the door open and all of those who were oppressed and captive and sick gathered at the door. The door that would normally be closed to keep people out, was now open to bring good news. Jesus preached the Good News about the Kingdom of God and He healed the sick and set the captives free – just like He said He would, back in the synagogue in Nazareth.

He threw the doors of the *oikos* open and showed what it is like to be a family on mission. He defined His mission, the mission of the *oikos* and, therefore, our mission when He said – *'The Son of Man came to seek and save the lost'.*

Mary, Jesus' mother, and His half-brothers heard what was happening and so they came to Capernaum later to take charge of Jesus. They thought that He was mad! When they arrived, they found an *oikos* full of people, maybe seventy-two people, all listening to Jesus. This had become something of a disciple making centre.

Chapter 11

'Gospel-ing'

'...I am not ashamed of the gospel, because it is the power of God that brings salvation to everyone who believes...'

Romans 1:16

The Apostle Paul wrote these words to the church in Rome, a church in the capital city of the Empire that ruled over the known world at the time. The Romans, and the Roman Empire, had put some things in place that really helped the spread of the Gospel in those early years of the life of the church,

- The *'Pax Romana'* – relative peace within the boundaries of the Empire.
- The common language of Greek which made communication across the Empire much easier.
- The Roman road system that helped travel.

However, this was a culture that did not believe that there was only one God, but many ways to many gods. They believed that Caesar, not Jesus, was Lord. This was a culture of promiscuity and lust for power. It was into the focal point of all of this that the Apostle Paul writes his letter to the followers of Jesus in Rome. This was not a church he had planted, but one that he hoped to visit. Chapter 16 helps us to see that they operated as a church which was scattered in *oikos* or household size groups, of up to 60 people each, around the city. Paul doesn't address any major errors or quarrels within the letter to the Romans, as he does in other of his letters. What he seems to do is to send his message, the Gospel – the truth that he preached, to them and so, in this pagan, idolatrous, synchronistic, promiscuous culture, Paul clearly, lovingly and boldly says:

> *'...I am not ashamed of the gospel, because it is the power of God that brings salvation to everyone who believes...'*
>
> Romans 1:16

We live in a world that tells us that there are many ways to many gods. That you, as an individual, are Lord – not Jesus. It tells us that promiscuity is okay and that truth is personal and not absolute. We live in a post Christian culture. One writer and thinker said that 'we are back in Rome'. (Though some are now beginning to ask if we are entering a phase where we are back to being pre-Christian. If post-Christian is cynical and somewhat hostile, pre-Christian is enquiring and questioning). Add to that the fact that, as believers, we often battle with doubts, fears, identity issues, we can struggle with unforgiveness and pride. Can we say confidently, with the Apostle Paul,

> *'...I am not ashamed of the gospel, because it is the power of God that brings salvation to everyone who believes...'* ?
>
> Romans 1:16

I believe that we can – the good news is still good news, and we don't need to be ashamed or embarrassed about it. The gospel that saved us, is the gospel that will keep us and, in the end, the gospel that we rely upon on the final day – the gospel is the *'Time Traveller's Passport'*. That begs the question, "What is the gospel?"

The Gospel

The word simply means 'Good News' and we find it used over 90 times in the New Testament. William Barclay, in his excellent commentary on the book of Romans, tells us that 'Gospel' comes from a Greek word *'Evangelion'*, which is used in both noun and verb form. It is derived from the word *'Angelos'*, which is often translated as *'Messenger'*. This was a person who brought news of a victory, which brought joy to the people – it was not originally a 'religious' word.

Bill Hull in *Conversion and Discipleship: You Can't Have One Without The Other*, points out that when we read the word Gospel in the New Testament, it is often accompanied by other words; so we have,

- *'the Gospel of God'* Mark 1:14
- *'the Gospel of Jesus Christ'* Mark 1:1
- *'the Gospel of His Son'* Romans 1:9
- *'the Gospel of the kingdom'* Mark 4:23
- *'the Gospel of the grace of God'* Acts 20:24
- *'the Gospel of the glory of Christ'* 2 Corinthians 4:4
- *'the Gospel of peace'* Ephesians 6:15
- *'an eternal Gospel'* Revelation 14:6

> *For I am not ashamed of the gospel, because it is the power of God that brings salvation to everyone who believes: first to the Jew, then to the Gentile. For in the gospel the righteousness of God is revealed – a righteousness that is by faith from first to last, just as it is written: 'The righteous will live by faith.'*
>
> Romans 1:16-17

The gospel is in keeping with the nature and character of God. It shows us who He is and what He is like. We see it in the work of God from creation, all the way through to completion in the book of Revelation. This is the eternal gospel of the eternal God and it is good news that is to bring us great joy.

When you hear the word gospel, what you think? I wonder if we have reduced the gospel to something smaller than what it really is?

The gospel is the good news that saved, keeps saving and will save us. It is the news that God is love and God is holy. God is forgiving and God is just. It is good news for the whole of life – good news that sets us free from the power of sin and the captivity to destructive mind sets, habits and thought patterns and practices that we may think will never change. The gospel is the power of God for our salvation. This is the best and biggest news ever, yet so often we can be tempted to be ashamed of it, to keep it to ourselves, to see it as a personal matter that doesn't really have much relevance to people today. The truth is that the Gospel, this good news of a victory that brings everlasting joy, is what people most need to know.

What is the Gospel?

So, the story starts with God. He has always been there and always will be. He exists both inside of, and outside of, time. In fact, He created time! He is holy – He always is and does what is right.

We read in Genesis 1:1, that God created the heavens and the earth. Some scholars think that the first book of the Bible to be written down was the book of Job, even though Genesis records events that took place before the story of Job. In the book of Job, God gives us some helpful information about the context in which the creation story took place,

> *Brace yourself like a man; I will question you, and you shall answer me. Where were you when I laid the earth's foundation? Tell me, if you understand. Who marked off its dimensions?*

> *Surely you know! Who stretched a measuring line across it? On what were its footings set, or who laid its cornerstone – while the morning stars sang together and all the angels shouted for joy?*
>
> Job 38:3-7

So, as God was laying the foundations of the earth, the *'morning stars'* sang for joy in worship. Who are they? They are the angels. God made these before He made human beings. The angels worshipped God as He created.

We discover that some of these angels rebelled against God. Lucifer was an angel and the chief worship leader in Heaven, but instead of being content with his position, he didn't want to just be close to God: he wanted to *be* God. Lucifer led one third of the angels in his rebellion against God, but God overcame him and cast him and his followers out of His presence. Lucifer was given the name 'Satan', which means *'adversary'* or *'accuser'*.

Satan and the fallen angels, now called demons, are cast down to the earth. At this stage, the earth was in darkness and was chaotic. The good news is that, when we feel in the dark and our world is in chaos, God can work and do good things!

The story unfolds and God created a perfect environment in which people could live and flourish, with each new thing He created He said that it was good. What God does, reflects who God is. However, when He created people He said that it was not good that they should be alone, but then when there were two of them, He said that this was very good.

So, God made people in His own image, which is one reason why He hates idols, because we are those who visually represent Him. God made people to enjoy being with Him, to reproduce and to have meaningful work. He gave them a sense of identity, linked to their relationship with Himself.

What about you? How do you view yourself?

What makes you, you? Your self-image?

For many people in our world, this issue of identity is a big one. '*Who am I and how do I find that out?*'

The start of the story of the Gospel has some big things to say about that. I wonder what gives you a sense of self-worth? Do you even have a real sense of self-worth?

Tim Chester talks about the '4G's', and we see these in the creation story,

- He is Good – and He does things that are very good
- He is Great – He has the power to make everything
- He is Glorious – He is wonderful and adored
- He is Gracious – His kindness is clear to see

What did God say about people?

> *Then God said, 'Let us make mankind in our image, in our likeness, so that they may rule over the fish in the sea and the birds in the sky, over the livestock and all the wild animals, and over all the creatures that move along the ground.'*
>
> Genesis 1:26

You are made in the image of God! There is something of His goodness, greatness, glory and grace in you!

We read that God places two very significant trees in the Garden of Eden. Let's look at what the story says,

> *The Lord God made all kinds of trees grow out of the ground – trees that were pleasing to the eye and good for food. In the middle of the garden were the tree of life and the tree of the knowledge of good and evil.*

The Lord God took the man and put him in the Garden of Eden to work it and take care of it…And the Lord God commanded the man, 'You are free to eat from any tree in the garden; but you must not eat from the tree of the knowledge of good and evil, for when you eat from it you will certainly die.'

Genesis 2:9, 15-17

Adam and Eve had a relationship with God that was good. They were open with God and with one another, but then there are these two trees. The tree of the knowledge of good and evil and the tree of life. I think that these trees represent choice. It would seem that it is impossible to have a genuinely loving relationship when there is no choice. If one person is forced into a relationship with another, how can that be love? So, God creates the possibility of choice. He knew the consequences of that, but He wants a real loving relationship with people so much that He is willing to not have a relationship at all, rather than a false one.

Adam and Eve can choose to love God and trust what He says, or they can choose not to. Isn't it interesting that these two trees are placed, by God, in the centre of the Garden of Eden – not tucked away at the back of the garden, behind a very large hedge, but right in the middle of their world in full view – the element of choice is central. Will we choose to love and trust what God says or not? Adam and Eve had that choice and so do we. So, the Gospel has an element of choice in it.

God loves you. The pressure is off – you don't have to try to make Him love you, or try to earn His love. He already loves you. He has always loved you. You bear His image and you were made for relationship with Him and for healthy relationships with others. You don't need to feel like you're not good enough. You don't need to be alone. You have a Father in Heaven who loves you and is longing for a relationship with you. He has a family that He wants you to belong to and a mission that He wants you to enjoy being a part of. He wants to help you to know how to be you, and He wants to release you into meaningful and significant activity. He is good and His plans for you are good. Gospel – Good News!

What if we really believed that? There is power in the Gospel for those who really believe it. Now, I know that we are all sinners, and that Jesus makes the way for our restoration. We see that as the Gospel story unfolds. But, there is something of the image of God in all people.

Genesis 3 tells us that God would walk with Adam and Eve in the cool of the day – they enjoyed relationship. God gives lots of permission and a few parameters – the same is still true.

However, Adam and Eve do not believe God. They do not see Him as He really is and so break through the parameters that He sets, and face the consequences.

The Gospel begins in Genesis 1, not Genesis 3. The Gospel begins with a loving and holy God who made people for relationship with Himself, it does not begin with sin that separates.

We read, in Genesis 3:1-5, how the devil deceived the first humans by getting them to believe lies about the nature of God.

The devil is offering the opportunity to be *'As God'*, not *'Blessed by God'*. He says that you can *'Be Lord'*, not just *'Be blessed by the Lord'*. Satan brought into question the nature of God. He questioned what God is really like and so sowed seeds of doubt about the nature of God and, therefore, the activity of God. This made Eve doubt her own identity and therefore disobey God.

We read, in Genesis 3:6, that an appetite was prompted that was satisfied independently from God. It is as if Adam and Eve are on the throne that God has given to them to rule from (not a literal throne). The devil offers them something but, as they reach out to take it, they have to step off the throne. As they look back to the throne, they see that the devil has sat on it – therefore he can offer the kingdoms of the world later in the Temptation of Jesus.

We then read, in Genesis 3:6-13, the results of this catastrophic decision. Sin crashed into the human experience. A new power was now at work in humanity which would lead us to make wrong choices; a bias to selfishness was now inbuilt. Along with this came fear, guilt and shame. But, the Good News, the Gospel, is that God has a plan,

> *And I will put enmity between you and the woman, and between your offspring and hers; he will crush your head, and you will strike his heel.*
>
> Genesis 3:15

This points to the coming of Jesus. Again and again, throughout the Old Testament, there are numerous prophecies that point to Jesus. The book of Hebrews makes it clear that the whole sacrificial system points to Him as the spotless one, both priest and sacrifice, who would properly deal with sin and make the way for us to be right with God. People in the Old Testament entered into a relationship with God by looking forward to this in faith, and we enter into a relationship with God by looking back, relying upon Him and His work on the cross and in the resurrection by faith.

> *The Word (Jesus) became flesh and blood, and moved into the neighbourhood...*
>
> John 1:14 (The Message)

God the Son moves into the neighbourhood. He gets involved; becomes one of us. If you want to know what God is like, then look at Jesus. How does God feel about the hungry? Look at Jesus feeding the five thousand. How does God feel about our pain and grief? Look at Jesus weeping at the grave of Lazarus. How does God feel about our sickness? Look at both the compassion and power of Jesus when He meets the sick. How does God feel about the excluded? Look at Jesus interacting with those that others had written off. How does God feel about our sin? Look at Jesus dying on the cross. How does God feel about people like you and me? Look at Jesus rising from the dead so that we can have a fresh start and everlasting life – Jesus is God, present in the world with His words and deed, communicating with us the truth about God for us all to see and know. Good News – Gospel.

> *Now, brothers and sisters, I want to remind you of the gospel I preached to you, which you received and on which you have taken your stand. By this gospel you are saved, if you hold firmly to the word I preached to you. Otherwise, you have believed in vain. For what I received I passed on to you as of first importance: that Christ died for our sins according to the Scriptures, that He was buried, that He was raised on the third day according to the Scriptures.*
>
> 1 Corinthians 15:1-4

Paul reminds us of the power of the gospel. He emphasises three important things,

- *'…Christ died for our sins according to the Scriptures,"* – the death of Jesus is the most significant death in the whole of human history. Why? "*God made him who had no sin to be sin for us, so that in him we might become the righteousness of God,'* 2 Corinthians 5:21. Jesus died to pay a price that we could not pay, so that we could receive a gift that we could not earn. This is the good news – the Gospel of Grace. There is nothing more that we could do to make ourselves right with God. We simply believe on the finished work of Jesus.

As He died, Jesus cried out, 'paid in full'. There is nothing we could add to His complete work.

- *'…he was buried...'* Why is this included? It is to verify that Jesus was really dead. He did not swoon or feign His death. He was really dead and buried.

- *'…he was raised on the third day...'* The resurrection of Jesus has massive implications in the Gospel story. It is an event in history that tells us that sin is properly dealt with. You see, Romans tells us that the wages of sin is death, so death come into human history because of sin. The resurrection of Jesus demonstrates that the power of sin is broken and so, where death was once at work, now life has come.

We live in a world where there is so much pain and injustice. We have seen acts of terror on the streets of our own nation, as well as seeing horrific suffering around our world. If God loves people, why doesn't He just step in and stop it all? Why doesn't He act and sort it all out?

The fact is that one day He will, but He waits. Why? Because He loves people, and He wants as many of us as possible to enter into the friendship with Him that we are made for. But, one day God will call history to a halt. Jesus will return – 2 Peter 3:9.

In passages like Acts 17:31 and Matthew 25:31-46, we read that Jesus will return to judge humanity. This is a sobering thought, but one day we all will have to give an account. The basis of this will be how we have responded to the claims of Jesus.

The Gospel story, in the Bible, begins in a Garden in Genesis and ends in a Garden City in the Book of Revelation. This is where we are heading. We are citizens of that city and the good news is that, in that place,

> *He will wipe every tear from their eyes. There will be no more death or mourning or crying or pain, for the old order of things has passed away.*
>
> Revelation 21:4

This Gospel is a Gospel of grace, from first to last. It has saved us, is saving us day by day, moment by moment. As we travel through time as disciples who make disciples, the gospel is our travelling companion. It is the means by which we can live as, and make disciples of Jesus. This Gospel will save us in the end. The Gospel is our confidence before God, and it is intrinsically linked to who He is, and so we are secure.

'…The Gospel…is the Power of God That…' Romans 1:16

The word for 'power' here, is *'dunamis'*. It means 'might', 'ability' – from this we get the word 'dynamite'. The Gospel is a demonstration of the explosive power of God. It blasts out of the way everything that could separate you from Him and empowers us to live the life that God invites us into, as His children.

Look at what Paul prays for the disciples in Ephesus,

> *I keep asking that the God of our Lord Jesus Christ, the glorious Father, may give you the Spirit of wisdom and revelation, so that you may know him better. I pray that the eyes of your heart may be enlightened in order that you may know the hope to which he has called you, the riches of his glorious inheritance in his holy people, and his incomparably great power for us who believe. That power is the same as the mighty strength he exerted when he raised Christ from the dead and seated him at his right hand in the heavenly realms, far above all rule and authority, power and dominion, and every name that is invoked, not only in the present age but also in the one to come. And God placed all things under his feet*

and appointed him to be head over everything for the church.

Ephesians 1:17-22

There is power in the Gospel to overcome all things. Jesus is raised from the dead by the exerted power of the Father, and His same power is now at work in us, as we believe the Gospel. So, whatever power, challenge, mind-set, opposition, fear, doubt or hurt that stands before you right now, is not more powerful than the power that raised Christ from the dead, and that same power is now available to us in the Gospel. Is your Gospel too small? Is your Gospel compartmentalised into small expectations and little prayers, or do we believe the Gospel – the power of God released on our behalf, because of who He is?

Jesus made a remarkable promise to His disciples,

But you will receive power when the Holy Spirit comes on you; and you will be my witnesses in Jerusalem, and in all Judea and Samaria, and to the ends of the earth.

Acts 1:8

The word 'power' here is the same Greek word as in Romans 1:16 – 'dunamis' – dynamite. God the Holy Spirit wants to empower us to live in the power of the Gospel, so that we can live the life that Jesus promises. This is not us trying harder, or a New Year's resolution, this is the power of Almighty God demonstrated in the Gospel and made available to us in God the Holy Spirit to live as missionaries, disciples, children of God in the here and now. He tells us what to do and then clothes us with the ability to do it.

Finally, be strong in the Lord and in his mighty power.

Ephesians 6:10

What follows is a description of what we call 'the Armour of God', but note how Paul begins. We get to be strong in the power that God gives, not our own self will, our own hype or self-effort. We get to live in the good of the Gospel and so, then, we can stand our ground. We can keep hold of all the good things that God has promised and given to us. If you feel like you lost ground, then let the good news of the Gospel set you free to see just who God is and what He does. This will help you to see who you now are, not what your negative inner-narrative may say that you are, or your fixed and limited mind set may say that you are, but who God says that you are. As you believe what He says about you, you are set free by the power of the Gospel, to live in the power of the Holy Spirit and to do what He says.

The power of the Gospel saves us and goes on saving us, as we allow the truth to set us free. As I said earlier in the book, in 2002 I experienced severe burnout and I know that there is still a tendency in me to become very focused on the mission and work that we are involved in. That can mean that I find it difficult to switch off and do Sabbath and rest well at times. The truth is, 'God is great, so I don't need to be in control'.

A few years ago, I noticed (as did those around me) that I was drifting back into unhealthy work patterns. People from our leadership team began to help me to see and live out the Good News in that situation. We grow as disciples in community. So, Wendy McCarthy from our team, helped me to list everything that I was doing and involved with then we grouped and coloured activities. One group was things that I was called to do, and I needed to keep doing. Then, things that were part of my role that I needed to keep doing. Then, things that I was doing that I could hand over to other people – we set time frames for when this could happen. Then, things that I was doing that no one needed to do and therefore needed to stop as soon as possible. Chris Littler, from the team, took charge of organising my diary – I knew that I needed help with this when

I realised that I had agreed to see three different people in different places at the same time! Then, Ian Moore and Wendy met me for an hour each month where I could tell them how my work/life balance was going. Believing that God is great and so I don't need to be in control in practice, took community to implement. The Good News of the Gospel is that God has done the work and so we don't need to live driven lives. We rest in His grace and work from that place of rest. Where is your unbelief of the Gospel currently impacting your behaviour, and what steps could you take with others to move from unbelief to faith?

If we are to travel well as pilgrim time-travellers through the here and now, and on to where we are going, we are wise to stay close to the Gospel. We are also wise to 'Gospel' one another – to call each other on to believe the truth that sets us free and doubt the lies that cause us to get stuck in a moment.

Footnote: I have found *Story of God* by Caesar Kalinowski very helpful in expressing thoughts and ideas expressed in this chapter. He writes in his training: **Acknowledgments:** 'Several years ago I met a man in Africa named John Witte, a US missionary in Sudan at the time. Months later John told us the Story of God in about four hours one day and it forever changed my life. He trained us to teach using simple stories found in the Bible combined with powerful dialogue. John has become a trusted friend and mentor…Along the way God led me to learn and train with others to whom I am grateful for much of the ideas…Many thanks for your encouragement and partnership in this great gospel work must be given to John Witte, Michael Novelli, Dr. Grant Lovejoy, J.O. Terry, Avery Willis and the elders of Soma Communities in Tacoma. Thanks brothers!' – *Caesar Kalinowski*

Chapter 12

Direction of Travel

I do not have a great sense of direction. When we are travelling in the car, Jacky says that I am at my most dangerous when I think I know where I am going. As we travel through time, seeking to live as disciples who make disciples, how do we know the direction in which to travel?

I would suggest that, sometimes, we need to simply follow the apostolic impulse that God gives to us. That is to keep moving to try things; as Jim Collins, author of the book *Great by Choice* says, 'fire bullets and then fire cannon balls'. In other words, invest a little in something, try it and, if it is fruitful, invest more time, energy and resource. Some people call this, 'following the fruit'. This is a helpful thing and I think that this is what the Apostle Paul and his team did for most of the book of Acts, but then there was that unusual season when they didn't seem to know where to go and the usual apostolic method of simply moving to the next place, or next key centre of population, didn't seem appropriate.

> *Paul and his companions travelled throughout the region of Phrygia and Galatia, having been kept by the Holy Spirit from preaching the word*

> *in the province of Asia. When they came to the border of Mysia, they tried to enter Bithynia, but the Spirit of Jesus would not allow them to. So they passed by Mysia and went down to Troas. During the night Paul had a vision of a man of Macedonia standing and begging him, 'Come over to Macedonia and help us.' After Paul had seen the vision, we got ready at once to leave for Macedonia, concluding that God had called us to preach the gospel to them.*
>
> Acts 16:6-10 NIV

Paul seems to be a person who liked 'to be on the move', but here he is stopped and waiting to know what next.

The prophetic and the apostolic mixed together are powerful. Sometimes, God allows us to grind to a halt so that we will listen to His specific prophetic direction in a situation.

Marc Dupont says that, 'Prophecy is often a springboard into a pool of prayer.' Pete Greig helpfully points out that, 'The point of prayer is not the power that it releases but the Person that it reveals.'

Sometimes, God speaks, and He invites us into a phase of the journey where we get to humble ourselves to hear Him.

'*You Will See a Deer*'

It was October time and we were spending a few days away with family in the Lake District. One the first day of our stay, I was spending some time listening to God and I sensed Him say to me, *'You will see a deer'*. I have been visiting the Lake District regularly for thirty years or more and I have only ever seen a deer in the wild (not in a park or deer sanctuary) two or three times.

A few days later, as daylight was fading, we were driving past Thirlmere when, right in front of our car, a large stag ran across the road and down towards the lake. It was amazing. It was a magnificent animal, but I had no idea what the significance of this was. I was impressed by the fact that God knew the whereabouts of the wildlife and when we would cross paths, but I could not see what on earth this could mean.

I must admit that, after a few days, I was a little perplexed and mildly frustrated, not having a clue what to make of the event.

A little while later, I was having a meeting with one of the teams at King's. After the meeting, one lady asked to see me. She said that she had arrived at the meeting early and so decided to sit in her car outside and spend some time praying for me. I really appreciate when people do that. As she was praying, she thought that she should give the following passage of scripture to me:

> *The Sovereign Lord is my strength; He makes my feet like the feet of a deer, He enables me to tread on the heights...*
>
> Habakkuk 3:19 NIV

The beauty of following Jesus with others is that we get their wisdom in times like this. I was in a huddle with Paul Maconochie where I told them about the deer episode. Paul pointed out to me that God was trying to get my attention and was inviting me to seek Him. I had a choice. I could respond with pride, say that this clue was more difficult than any in *The Times* crossword, and say to God that when He was ready to speak clearly I was ready to listen, or I could humble myself and begin to give time and attention to seeking to hear just what God wanted to say. I chose the second response.

I shared these things with the Leadership Team at King's, who agreed to pray with me about what God might be saying. A few weeks later, Dan Curtis (one of the team) told us that he had been researching deer and stags and that the stags would sometimes go away from the others and be alone, or be even with other stags, and would later return.

The previous year, the Leadership Team had asked if I would like to take a sabbatical and I refused. Now they offered again, sensing that God was inviting us to step aside to seek Him for the next season on the journey and so, in 2016, I took my first (and up to now only) sabbatical. This was a period of three months, some alone and some with Jacky, to study, observe, listen, think, write and be renewed.

Our posture is so important as we seek to hear God. Not whether we are standing, sitting, kneeling or face down on the ground, but the posture of our attitude. James tells us that, *'God opposes the proud but shows favour to the humble.'* James 4:6 NIV. If we try to seek God, but we are proudly demanding that He speaks on our terms or in the way that we are used to, then we will find it difficult to hear Him. When we choose to humble ourselves, seek Him and be willing to listen to Him in any way in which He chooses to speak, then we will hear Him.

Indeed, Jesus promises that we will hear Him,

> *My sheep listen to my voice; I know them, and they follow me.*
>
> John 10:27 NIV
>
> *Humble yourselves, therefore, under God's mighty hand, that he may lift you up in due time.*
>
> 1 Peter 5:6 NIV

God wants us to be lifted up as His people, but He does not want us to do the lifting. As we humble ourselves before Him, He gives us the heads up on the way to go.

Three Phases of Hearing from God

When I was at Bible College, we had the privilege of having Colin Dye lecture us on the book of Acts. In his lectures, Colin told us that there are three phases to hearing from God:

Revelation – what is God saying? Sometimes, God speaks in very simple and clear ways and we immediately know what He is saying. For example, the work of restoration in the temple had come to a halt in the time of Haggai because the people had become distracted. The Word of the Lord came to Haggai that they should be strong and build, because God is with them. This was very clear, and everyone knew just what to do. So, revelation is, 'What did we hear?'

Interpretation – here the question is, 'What is God wanting to really say through what we hear?' So 'what does it mean?' There is a fascinating passage in Acts 21 that highlights this,

> *We sought out the disciples there and stayed with them seven days. Through the Spirit they urged Paul not to go on to Jerusalem. When it was time to leave, we left and continued on our way. All of them, including wives and children, accompanied us out of the city, and there on the beach we knelt to pray... After we had been there a number of days, a prophet named Agabus came down from Judea. Coming over to us, he took Paul's belt, tied his own hands and feet with it and said, 'The Holy Spirit says, "In this way the Jewish leaders in Jerusalem will bind the owner of this belt and will hand him over to the Gentiles."' When we heard this, we and the people there pleaded with Paul not to go up to Jerusalem. Then Paul answered, "Why are you weeping and breaking my heart? I am ready not only to be bound, but also to die in Jerusalem for the name of the Lord Jesus." When he would not be dissuaded, we gave up and said, "The Lord's will be done." After this, we started on our way up to Jerusalem."*
>
> Acts 21:4-5, 10-15

The first group of disciples had received some *revelation* that Paul would face a difficult time in Jerusalem, but they were not mature in the prophetic gift and so jumped to their own *interpretation* and *application* that God must not want Paul to go to Jerusalem. Then, as the journey continues, Paul meets Agabus who is a more mature prophet. Agabus seems to have the same Revelation as the earlier disciples, that Paul's visit to Jerusalem would be a challenging one. However, Agabus does not make a hasty *application*. He does not tell Paul what to do. He waits for the *interpretation*. Most of the time, a prophetic message to someone is a confirmation of, or fits in with, something that God has already been saying to them. God wanted Paul to go to Jerusalem and was assuring him that, even though there would be some challenges, God had gone ahead of him, God knew all about it and God would see him through.

We are wise to take time to wait on God for *application* as well as *revelation*. We are all learners and 1 Corinthians 13:9 tells us that, *'We know in part and we prophecy in part.'*

Application – in 1 Corinthians, we see that there are various prophetic gifts. So, a word of knowledge may give us *revelation* about a situation. We, or someone else, may then have a prophetic word that gives us insight and *interpretation* about that situation. Then, we, or someone else, may have a word of wisdom so that we know the *application* – what are we supposed to do.

Here are two highly important questions that we use in living as disciples who make disciples,

1. What is God saying to you?
2. What are you going to do about it?

Revelation leads to *interpretation* which, in turn, leads to *application*. We are part of a 'Family on Mission' as a church, in Missional Communities and in Missional Households. The phrase, 'Family on Mission', works on lots of levels. So, we don't need to try to work out what God is saying and what we are going to do about it alone – in fact it is best that we don't. We get to do this with others who love, and are following, Jesus too.

Caesar Kalinowski reminds us that a great question to ask is, 'What next Lord?' What is the next small step of obedience that God is asking you to take in this life long journey of growing in our character and gifting?

Lessons From The Journey

As part of the three-month sabbatical, Jacky and I travelled to Israel on *The Footsteps of Jesus* pilgrimage with Bob and Pam Rognlien. Here we were impacted by the humanity of Jesus the *'tekton'*. A *'tekton'* is a builder. Jesus is the builder, who became the stone that the builders rejected, who builds His church with living stones.

We were also immensely enriched and challenged by a visit to the USA. There, we spent some time with Crossroads Church in Cincinnati, and the Soma Churches in San Francisco and the Bay Area. We also had some time with John and Glenda Nordstrom, who lead Christ Community Church in Ottawa, Illinois.

We were also blessed to visit other churches in the UK and Europe in this season.

We met and had time with some amazing people who, in a variety of settings, were living as missionary disciples. They were contextualising the words, works and ways of Jesus and having a remarkable impact. They were using buildings but not being defined by them. They were learning the balance of professionalism and family, using different sized gatherings appropriately.

A phrase that we came away with was, *'Intentional but not intense'*. King's has always been a people of focus, fun and laughter. We needed to guard this and see it develop.

We also had a renewed sense of the love and concern in God's heart for the poor but didn't really know what to do with this.

When we take time to step back and learn from others, some who are like us and others who are not, we get to see more of who God is. It can be so tempting to make God in our own image, so in our thinking we believe that He always agrees with us or sees things the way that we do. The truth is that we are made in His image, and He is about the work, over time, of shaping us into the people that He invites us to be. For us to stand any chance of making significant progress in this, we must adopt the posture of a learner who is willing to be flexible and pass on what we learn.

We re-entered after sabbatical with new eyes and new clarity. We moved lots of our leaders gatherings back into our home. I remember walking into the venue that we had been using for our Sunday gatherings for years, and sensing it was time to move. Jacky and I shared this with the leaders and expected a season of transition and preparation. But, within weeks, we had received an email from the school telling us that, due to some changes at the school, we could no longer rent the venue and had four weeks to find somewhere else.

I opened the email telling us this, just as I finished writing a talk about the Sovereignty of God. I knew that we had an opportunity to trust Him for a new season.

Jacky was visiting our daughter and, soon to be, son-in-law and his family in Germany when the news arrived about the venue. The next morning, they prayed together, and Jacky sent us a sketch of King's gathering in five Bases: north, south, east, west and central. We discussed this as a team but didn't feel ready for this so, after lots of searching, found another venue and met in two groups – one in the east on Sunday afternoon, and one in the west of the town on Sunday morning, coming together every month or so. All of this was with Missional Communities continuing to function.

A year later, we moved from the larger morning venue and closed the afternoon gathering. We again explored the five Bases idea but didn't do it. A year later, we almost lost the morning venue again. We decided that we needed to act on the prophetic word, even though we didn't feel ready and so we began a rhythm of gathering in three Bases and a central celebration on different weeks of the month, with Missional Communities, Missional Households, Huddles still providing spaces for life as Family on Mission.

When God speaks to us prophetically, He finds a way of keeping bringing us back to the point where we can choose to do what He says. We are wise to respond quickly if we want to keep moving forwards.

We are still learning how to operate and multiply Bases well. However, I am convinced that we learn best in the context of practice, as we travel together on mission. We didn't feel ready, but we followed what we believed God was directing us to do.

Timing and Edges

The future phase of the journey is often on the fringe and edges of the present. We had returned from sabbatical with a concern for the poor in our town, and had done some things over the following years, but we felt that we were not making the impact that we had hoped for.

In 2020, the world was shaken in many ways by the global Covid 19 pandemic, the evil of racism and economic inequality being magnified by the crisis. We were concerned that families in our town, who were financially struggling, would be severely impacted. As schools were impacted, what would happen to children who relied on free school meals? Mike and Julieanna Ryder are leaders at King's and had just taken over Resonate Missional Community. They were in the process of refocusing the mission field of the Missional Community to the area where they live, which is an area of social and economic need in the town. In the geographical footprint between their home and the Chapelford Base, there are one thousand children living in poverty.

As a Missional Community, they were beginning to wonder about how they could begin to serve and reach out to their area. As the pandemic hit, Mike led the way in setting up a service area in King's that was named *'King's Table'*, where we would collect and donate food and then distribute it to families in need in the area. Within eight weeks, food had been delivered to families on every street in the area that Resonate were seeking to serve and reach.

Collaboration between Resonate and our social media team, online celebration, other Missional Communities, Missional Households, families, schools, neighbours and local organisations, enabled the idea of serving those in financial and practical need to become a living reality.

The activity that starts small, seems to take time and is connected to what is happening already, but which is new and different, is often the pathway that God is leading us along as we head into the future. Hearing and obeying involve a posture of humility and interdependency, moving from *me* to *we*.

Chapter 13

Need a Little Time to Wake Up

One of the Government's slogans in the Covid 19 pandemic was 'Stay Alert'. What is the point in the day when are you most alert?

I need a little time to wake up. I don't mind getting up early, but I take some time to gain focus. Jacky, on the other hand, is at her best first thing in the morning. She wakes up at 100mph, full of ideas, thoughts, questions and dreams. I just want coffee, a shower, prayer and time alone. I don't even like to eat for at least an hour after waking up. When we were first married, Jacky was convinced that she could break me out of my easing into the day. She would tell me that, as soon as my eyes open, I should just get out of bed and get going. So, one day in our second year of marriage, (I took some convincing that this was a good idea) I did it. I woke up, my eyes opened, I got out of bed and walked straight into the wardrobe. I managed to make my way out of the bedroom and then fell downstairs. Jacky now gives me time to wake up – Romans 8:28 in action!

One of my favourite proverbs, written by the wisest man in the whole of the Old Testament, is,

> *If anyone loudly blesses their neighbour early in the morning, it will be taken as a curse.*
>
> Proverbs 27:14 NIV

So, if you are a morning person, good for you but please keep quiet about it.

The thing about being asleep is that you don't know that you are asleep. As Stan Laurel once said, 'I was dreaming I was awake and woke up and found myself asleep.'

As we travel through time, it is so easy to drift onto autopilot and snooze. We can miss days, weeks and even years of growing as disciples and making disciples by sleeping on the job.

In Luke 9, Jesus took Peter, James and John with Him up onto a mountain to pray and, while He was praying, His appearance changed, and He was transfigured before them.

> *Peter and his companions were very sleepy, but when they became fully awake, they saw his glory...*
>
> Luke 9:32 NIV

Peter, James and John were with Jesus, but they were not fully awake. However, when they woke up, they saw something more of the glory and the purpose of Jesus.

If we are travelling through time, one day at a time, growing as disciples who make disciples, then we need to be alert, awake to what God is saying to us and what we are going to do about that.

It is possible for us to simply pass through time and our appearance, fashion sense, energy levels and appearance change, but for our development as a disciple to be sealed in a time capsule. We fall asleep or get stuck. We stop walking forwards and stand still, then sit down, then lie down and then drift off – life moves on, and we stay still.

There are numerous things that can cause us to stop moving forwards, to fall asleep and ultimately get stuck.

When we change focus from Jesus to ourselves, we are likely to get stuck. The disappointments and hurts that life brings to us all can either be processed with the help of God, His word, His people and His grace, or they can become sticking points that define us and halt our progress as disciples of Jesus. Consumerism is a dominant force in western culture, and it can lead to us being deceived into the pursuit of possessions and comfort which, in the end, possess and limit us. The potential to be distracted, to give time and energy to other things more than following Jesus, can lead to spiritual drift, lethargy and sleepiness.

The Apostle Paul says,

> *Wake up, sleeper, rise from the dead, and Christ will shine on you.*
>
> Ephesians 5:14 NIV

How do we do this? What are the wake up calls?

The love of God motivates Him to speak to us, to awaken us from our sleep, and get us moving again,

> *The Sovereign Lord has given me a well-instructed tongue, to know the word that sustains the weary. He wakens me morning by morning, wakens my ear to listen like one being instructed.*
>
> Isaiah 50:4 NIV

Suffering can act as a wake-up call. CS Lewis, in *The Problem of Pain*, said,

> We can ignore even pleasure. But pain insists upon being attended to. God whispers to us in our pleasures, speaks in our conscience, but shouts in

> our pains: it is His megaphone to rouse a deaf world…

Acts 2 records a significant awakening in the history of the church. It was the Feast of Pentecost. Pentecost literally means 'fifty'. It is fifty days from Passover. In the Old Testament, the feast was a celebration – the spring harvest period, also known as the Feast of Weeks. In the New Testament, we remember that Jesus died and rose again at the Feast of Passover and, when the disciples were empowered by the Holy Spirit fifty days later, there was the beginnings of a 'harvest' of people becoming followers of Jesus – an awakening began.

God wants to awaken and empower people with the Holy Spirit. We don't just get to know about God, we get to encounter Him.

God is so generous, and He loves to give good gifts, but not only does He love to give good gifts, He loves to give Himself to us,

> *So I say to you: Ask and it will be given to you; seek and you will find; knock and the door will be opened to you. For everyone who asks receives; the one who seeks finds; and to the one who knocks, the door will be opened. Which of you fathers, if your son asks for a fish, will give him a snake instead? Or if he asks for an egg, will give him a scorpion? If you then, though you are evil, know how to give good gifts to your children,* ***how much more will your Father in heaven give the Holy Spirit to those who ask him!***
>
> Luke 11:9-13 NIV

When we ask God for the Holy Spirit, He gives us the Holy Spirit. We get to have confidence in the Word of God and the generosity of God. We get to remember that God is more capable of keeping His word than the devil is of deceiving us.

We do not earn the infilling of the Holy Spirit. He is given as a gift. As we encounter Him, we become increasingly awake to things as they really are.

As Christians, we believe in the Holy Trinity: God the Father, God the Son and God the Holy Spirit. They are co-equal and co-eternal. They are one God. I guess, a bit like in our mind we have our will (the ability to choose), our emotions (the ability to feel) and our intellect (the ability to reason) but we only have one mind.

Broadly speaking, the different roles within the Trinity are as follows,

- The Father initiates
- The Son carries out the will of the Father
- The Holy Spirit applies this to people

A Little Time To Wake Up: Acts 1 – Ten Days From Ascension To Pentecost

Often, life throws up for us disappointments, shocks and let downs that we did not anticipate. I guess none of us saw what 2020 had in store for us!

I don't think the disciples were fully awake to the implications of what happened with Judas' betrayal and Jesus' death and resurrection, even though Jesus had warned them.

How do you deal with setbacks? What do you do when there is the potential to get stuck and to drift off into a debilitating sleep? When an issue arises that saddens and disappoints you, do you camp there for weeks, months, years? You may be stuck in a moment that happened twenty years ago. Your life has moved on, but your walk with God is on hold. How do you wake up and move on?

The disciples, in Acts 1, did some very simple but effective things that made a real difference. They regrouped, they obeyed

Jesus' words, and they stuck together. Acts 1:14 –*'They all joined together constantly...'* The temptation is to isolate and to hide – even to hide in plain sight. So, we may even continue to attend church gatherings, but stay on the edge. If you want to wake up, then regroup.

Over the years of leadership, I have heard many people say that they are going to take time out from gathering with other believers. Some even say that God has told them to do this. God will never tell you to do something that the Bible expressly forbids,

> *And let us consider how we may spur one another on toward love and good deeds, not giving up meeting together, as some are in the habit of doing, but encouraging one another – and all the more as you see the Day approaching.*
>
> Hebrews 10:24-25 NIV

It never ends well when we isolate ourselves from other followers of Jesus. I have yet to meet anyone who has done this and have later reconnected more awake and spiritually alive. The church is not a group of perfect people. It is a community, where we will be hurt and disappointed at times. However, it is the best environment for us to grow as missionary disciples and to work out the 'one another' instructions of the Bible.

They prayed: Acts 1:14 *'They all joined together constantly in prayer...'* Nic Harding often says, 'Prayer is where the heavy lifting is done'. It was in this season of prayer that the Holy Spirit fell upon them and they were propelled into a new and fruitful season of life. There was another prayer meeting in Acts 4, which took place following a season of opposition and persecution. The result again was that the disciples were filled with the Holy Spirit.

> *When they heard this, they raised their voices together in prayer to God...*
>
> Acts 4:24

> *After they prayed, the place where they were meeting was shaken. And they were all filled with the Holy Spirit and spoke the word of God boldly.*
>
> Acts 4:31

The result was that the story in the whole city changed – an awakening took place. In Acts 1 the whole city had been talking about the betrayal of Judas,

> *With the payment he received for his wickedness, Judas bought a field; there he fell headlong, his body burst open and all his intestines spilled out.* ***Everyone in Jerusalem heard about this****, so they called that field in their language Akeldama, that is, Field of Blood.*
>
> Acts 1:18-19 NIV

Now, the religious authorities who were persecuting the disciples gave this assessment of the situation,

> *'We gave you strict orders not to teach in this name,' he said. 'Yet you have filled Jerusalem with your teaching and are determined to make us guilty of this man's blood.'*
>
> Acts 5:28

As we pray with others, we begin to wake up and the impact of this begins to reach beyond us.

Prayer is not just us reciting our words to God. He speaks to us and we get to hear what God says and act on it. Life throws up some difficult situations, but we get to stay awake and keep going and as we go make disciples. It is not that we become harsh and unfeeling, but we learn to hear God and trust in His goodness; even when all around us doesn't seem good. Peter helped the other disciples to have a perspective from the Bible, so that they could keep going.

...Brothers and sisters, the Scripture had to be fulfilled in which the Holy Spirit spoke long ago through David concerning Judas, who served as guide for those who arrested Jesus...

Acts 1:16

If we simply allow our disappointment or confusion to reign, it can either lull us into a place of apathy, inactivity and sleep, or cause us to react and respond in an unhealthy way, from a place of hurt.

If we are going to keep moving and 'As we go make disciples', then the Word of God will have to be the lens through which we interpret the events of life. It helps us to know the truth, and the truth sets us free. It is so easy to stop, settle down and drift off; to get stuck when we begin to believe lies about ourselves, God or others. Those early disciples could have spent years asking why God allowed the events around the suicide of Judas to happen. They could have allowed that to warp and twist their view of the nature of God and to see Him as harsh, uncaring and cruel. But instead, God's Word helped them to see the loving redemptive plan of a holy and just God. What is God saying to you in His Word that will help you to stay awake, to keep going and make disciples?

If we are to be fully awake, then we need to deal with the issues that caused us to fall asleep. The disciples, in Acts 1, dealt with the issue,

Then they prayed, 'Lord, you know everyone's heart. Show us which of these two you have chosen to take over this apostolic ministry, which Judas left to go where he belongs.' Then they cast lots, and the lot fell to Matthias; so he was added to the eleven apostles.

Acts 1:24-26

The work of disciple making was of such importance that setbacks, even as difficult and painful as they are, would not stop them. They dealt with the issue and kept moving. Are you allowing an issue, a pain or disappointment to keep you stuck in a moment? Are you often replaying it in your thinking and discussing it with others, looking for sympathy and support? Do you want to wake up and keep moving? If so, regroup with followers of Jesus, pray, discover what the Bible says you should do, take courage, deal with the issue and keep moving. Keep making disciples as you go.

Suddenly In The Process: Acts 2

Being a disciple, or a follower of Jesus, is a process but, in that process, there are *'suddenlys'*. Times when things significantly move, shift and step forward. Acts 2 describes one of those *'suddenly'* moments,

> *When the day of Pentecost came, they were all together in one place.* ***Suddenly*** *a sound like the blowing of a violent wind came from heaven and filled the whole house where they were sitting. They saw what seemed to be tongues of fire that separated and came to rest on each of them.*
>
> Acts 2:1-3 NIV

They were now awake and were about to be propelled into a new season. Discipleship involves us navigating unchartered territory with the Word of God, the Spirit of God and the People of God.

What Happened?

'*There was the sound of a violently blowing wind' v2*

The Hebrew word for Spirit is, *'ruach'*. The Greek word is, *'pneuma'*. Both mean *'breath'* or *'wind'*. It is the word used when God breathed His life into Adam, back in the book of Genesis. Here in Acts 2, we see Him breathing the empowering, awakening breath of His Spirit into the church.

Sometimes, when the Spirit moves, there are physical manifestations. We feel something or see something happen. Like when a tree is blown by the wind and bends, the bending tree is not the wind; it is the visible evidence that the wind is blowing. Clearly something was happening to the 120, as people accused them of being drunk – not the usual accusation for speaking in another language.

Sometimes when the Spirit moves, people are overwhelmed, they cannot stand up or they weep or feel amazing joy. The experiences are not to be the focus. The focus must be God. How do we know if the feeling or experience is from God? After all, the devil can make people fall, laugh, cry etc., as can emotionalism. So, how do we know that it is God? By the fruit. Jonathan Edwards, a theologian and church leader from Northampton, New England, lived in the 1700s and saw an amazing move of the Holy Spirit. He wrote a booklet entitled, *A Thesis Concerning Religious Affections,* in which he points out that the true test of whether an experience is the Holy Spirit at work can only truly be known by the fruit that it produces.

Galatians says,

> *But the fruit of the Spirit is love, joy, peace, forbearance, kindness, goodness, faithfulness, gentleness and self-control. Against such things there is no law.*
>
> Galatians 5:22-23

The fruit of the blowing of the violent wind can be seen clearly throughout the rest of Acts 2.

Tongues of Fire v3

God is both Love and Holy. Fire, in the Bible, is a powerful symbol of both purity and love. When the Holy Spirit comes, He wants to burn up all of the rubbish that can clutter up our lives, because He loves us. The Bible says things like,

> *...Our God is a consuming fire.*
>
> Hebrews 12:29

> *...for love is as strong as death...It burns like a blazing fire, like a mighty flame.* That can be translated, *'like the very flame of the Lord.'*
>
> Song of Songs 8:6

> *.. who can endure the day of his coming? Who can stand when he appears? For he will be like a refiner's fire or a launderer's soap. He will sit as a refiner and purifier of silver; he will purify the Levites and refine them like gold and silver. Then the Lord will have men who will bring offerings in righteousness.*
>
> Malachi 3:2-3

When the Holy Spirit is at work in our lives, He turns the heat up on sin. He refines us and asks us to live differently. He does this because He loves us, and He wants us to live the life for Him that we could live. Fire purifies and 'sets on fire'.

Speaking in Tongues v4

> *All of them were filled with the Holy Spirit and began to speak in other tongues as the Spirit enabled them.*
>
> Acts 2:4

This is an important aspect of the events of the Day of Pentecost. The gift of tongues can be a very helpful gift to help us to build ourselves up as disciples and thus to stay awake and keep moving. Let's briefly look at some questions around this gift:

- Does everyone who is filled with the Holy Spirit speak in tongues? In my view, not everyone who is filled with the Holy Spirit speaks in tongues, but it seems like most do.

- What is the purpose of the personal use of speaking in tongues? As we speak in tongues in our personal conversation with God, we build ourselves up in our faith. The gift of tongues also helps us to pray and worship – 1Corinthians 14:4; Romans 8:26-27.
- What about the public use of the gift of tongues? If there is a 'message in tongues' in a public gathering, then we are to expect an interpretation. This is not a word for word translation, but more like a thought for thought interpretation – 1 Corinthians 14:13; 14:26.
- Can we speak in tongues in corporate worship and prayer? Yes, I believe that we can. We are not addressing the gathering but rather speaking or singing to God – Ephesians 6:18.
- When people speak in tongues, is it always a known language? I Corinthians 13:1 talks about us speaking with the tongues of men and angels, so both known and unknown languages are used.

Courage to Break Forth

Somewhere between Acts 2:4 and 5, they burst out of the upper room and out into the public place. The doors opened and the message spilled out to those outside who needed to hear.

'The seedbed of the future is incubated in the present.'

We could see the upper room as being a bit like a womb. It was a place of nurture and growth, but then birth had to happen. What had, at one time, been life giving was now restrictive and needed to change. The awakening in the upper room led to lots of people waking up to the reality of the risen Jesus and the birthing of outward looking missional households all over Jerusalem and beyond.

Breaking forth, like birth, can be uncomfortable, painful and messy – but it is worth it.

Without oxen the stable stays clean, but you need a strong ox for a large harvest.

Proverbs 14:4 NLT

A messy stable can be a sign of harvest. We need to put up with the messiness of birth and new life. Then there follows a season where there is more order and growth. This is followed by a messy season again as there is a break forth into new harvest fields. When toddlers are awake, nurseries can be messy and frustrating but there is life, order and growth that will come. If you want somewhere where there is always neatness and never the messiness of new life, then visit the local cemetery. Everything is ordered in nice rows, but there is no life!

When we feel in a season of restriction, it can be self-imposed, or even the enemy attacking us. It could be that we are beginning to realise that it is time to wake up and move on. It can also be that we have grown to our potential in this season and we are ready to break forth into a new season. Either way, the Holy Spirit can empower us for this new territory.

Throughout the book of Acts, we see the Holy Spirit awakening and empowering the people of God to break forth with the mission of God. He is constantly at work with them, removing barriers so that Acts 1:8 will be fulfilled.

The book of Acts records a thirty year period, where the mission of being disciples who make disciples moved from Jerusalem, to Judea, to Samaria and even reached the capital of the then known world – Rome.

What Shall We Do? Acts 2:38

When the people heard this, they were cut to the heart and said to Peter and the other apostles, 'Brothers, what shall we do?' Peter replied, 'Repent and be baptised, every one of you, in the

> *name of Jesus Christ for the forgiveness of your sins. And you will receive the gift of the Holy Spirit. The promise is for you and your children and for all who are far off – for all whom the Lord our God will call.'*
>
> Acts 2:37-39 NIV

What do we need to do? Here we find three simple foundations, launch pads for the journey, as followers of Jesus:

- Repent – become a follower of Jesus.
- Be baptised – to plunge, sink or immerse. As followers of Jesus, we die to one way of living and are resurrected to another. Baptism is a public burial of that old way of living.
- Receive the gift of the Holy Spirit.

Who is this for? What does the Bible say? For those who were there in Jerusalem on that day and for their children. Also, for people who were alive at the time and lived in other places, and for all. Did you notice that? All whom the Lord will call. There are some people who claim that the gift of the ongoing infilling of the Holy Spirit is not for today. That is not what the Bible says. What we see here is that the Bible tells us that the gift of the infilling of the Holy Spirit is for all whom the Lord will call. If you are a follower of Jesus, then this gift is available for you. In fact, it is a vital component to staying awake and keeping moving.

A New Community

What does it look like in practice, to live wide awake? To be publicly identified as a follower of Jesus?

> *They devoted themselves to the apostles' teaching and to fellowship, to the breaking of bread and to prayer. Everyone was filled with awe at the many wonders and signs performed by the apostles. All the believers were together and*

had everything in common. They sold property and possessions to give to anyone who had need. Every day they continued to meet together in the temple courts. They broke bread in their homes and ate together with glad and sincere hearts, praising God and enjoying the favour of all the people. And the Lord added to their number daily those who were being saved.

Acts 2:42-47

We get to share life with other followers of Jesus. Some we find it easy to be with, and others we may find it challenging to be with.

Look at the areas of life that being a disciple impacted,

- Devotion to the teaching of the Apostles.
- Devotion to the fellowship that they were a part of.
- Devotion to breaking bread together.
- Devotion to prayer.
- Seeing signs and wonders.
- How they handled their money and their goods.
- Regular large gatherings as a whole church.
- Regular meetings in their homes in mid-sized groups, where they enjoyed food together.
- Praising God.
- Daily, new disciples added.

There are times when this will be easy and times when it will be more difficult. The fruit, the result of an encounter with Jesus, is that we love the things that He loves and Jesus loves His church.

When we move to the edges or isolate ourselves because of busyness, hurt, disappointment etc., it is easy to fall asleep and get stuck in a moment; trapped in an issue, and to stall in our walk with God. However, when we show resilience and keep going in our commitment to one another, it helps us to keep moving and keep growing into all that we could be.

The Holy Spirit

- Gives us the comfort of belonging – Romans 8:15.
- Gives us the community of God's people – the unity of the Spirit – Ephesians 4:3.
- Gives us the courage to live wide awake as disciples who make disciples – Acts 1:8.

God loves you and He longs to fill you with His Holy Spirit, so that you can live fully awake, and courageously break forth into what He has next for you. You can be a disciple that makes disciples. You are a child of God. The Bible tells us that, *'...perfect love drives out fear...'* (1 John 4:18) and that love also helps us to have a healthy fear of God.

You may have been trapped by the fear of failure, the fear of what people will think, the fear of _______, well, you fill in the blank. God's love drives out fear. How do we get to experience that love?

> *...The love of God is shed abroad in our hearts by the Holy Spirit.*
>
> Romans 5:5

I urge you to wake up and to stay awake. To go on being filled with the Holy Spirit – Ephesians 5:18.

Chapter 14

Past and Future Shape the Present

We get to choose. We can live in the past, ignore the future and waste the present, or we can learn from the past, be present in the present and travel towards the future. Discipleship involves movement. Sometimes we feel like we can run and other times it is all that we can do to put one foot in front of the other, but as we go, as we press on and we travel through time, we make disciples.

Learn From The Past

The past is important and how we view it can shape our future. Some people only remember the good things from the past, 'The good old days', and view everything through rose coloured spectacles. Others only see their past failures and disappointments and allow these to limit their future.

There is a place for 'remembering' the past. In the Old Testament, God tells the Hebrew people to '*remember*' – Deuteronomy 24:18; 15:15; 7:18; Numbers 15:40 amongst other places. The Hebrew people are told to *remember* how God set them free from slavery in Egypt, *remember* how He led them through the Red Sea, *remember* His laws and commandments.

They even, at times, set up piles of stones in certain geographical places to remind them of God's work, such as crossing the River Jordan (Joshua 4:1-4).

So, you can imagine their shock when, in Isaiah He says,

> *Forget the former things; do not dwell on the past. See I am doing a new thing! Now it springs up; do you not perceive it? I am making a way in the wilderness and streams in the wasteland...*
>
> Isaiah 43:18-19

So, are we meant to remember or forget? Yes.

The problem occurs when we forget the things that we are supposed to remember and remember the things that we are supposed to forget.

God had reminded them of how He had parted the sea and made a way, but now they had to learn from the past and not live there. There are principles that are eternal, but some actions and practices that are bespoke to the moment.

They had to 'forget' and 'remember' appropriately about parting a sea because they were now in a wilderness and, instead of parting a sea, God was 'making a way' and providing 'streams'. How we respond to the present can be informed by our past experiences of God but must not lead us to trying to replicate the past.

I want to remember the past and thank God for all His work amongst us but, in a way like the Apostle Paul, we also need to forget it,

> *Forgetting what is behind and straining towards what is ahead, I press on...*
>
> Philippians 3:13-14

God has a future for us, and we can't take hold of it if we are trying to live in the past. We must learn from the past but not live there.

As we move into the future as King's Church, we are always about ABCDE. We are always about 'Having a deep relationship with God and sharing Him with others.' We are always about being 'Disciples who make disciples.' But we will keep on changing, growing and developing because that is what healthy living things do! Families change, develop and mature, but they remain family.

If that is thc casc for a church, how about for you as an individual? Are you going to allow your failures and disappointments from the past limit and define your future? Are you going to let the successes and glories of the past be seen as the high-water mark in your life and live as if your best days are behind you? As a follower of Jesus, we must always remember that the best days are still ahead of us and our past does not have to limit, or define, our future, no matter what people say to us or you say to yourself!

Be Present In The Present

Living in the present can be very difficult for us. It is easier to remember the past and dream about the future, but what about here and now?

In Philippians, we see that the Apostle Paul is very focused on what he is doing now. He knows that God has taken hold of him for something and he is determined to take hold of that too.

> *I press on to take hold of that for which Christ Jesus took hold of me...*
>
> Philippians 3:12

Living in the present requires us to be present – to be focused and attentive to what the Holy Spirit is asking us to do now.

Again, the two key discipleship questions that will define how we handle the present are:

- *What is God saying to you at this point in your life?*
- *What are you going to do about that?*

Discipleship is about *transformation;* becoming more and more the person that God is inviting us to be and seeing more of HIS Kingdom at work in us and through us.

Dallas Willard says,

> Discipleship is the process of becoming who Jesus would be if He were you.

It is important that we know what Jesus says and it is vital that we do what Jesus says. The problem, sometimes, is not that we don't know what Jesus is saying – it is that we don't follow through and do it.

Perhaps God has asked you to do something and you haven't got round to doing it or have just refused. When that happens, the sense of travelling purposefully through time stops and we get bored. The temptation then can be to make the mistake of thinking that what we need is more information. So we look for 'deeper' teaching that tells us where everyone else is going wrong, or we crave more interesting facts and details about the context of the Bible. Let me be clear, I want to understand, the best that I can, the historical, sociological, political, geographical contexts of scripture, but they are no substitute for doing what you already know God is asking us to do. When we act on what He says, we keep moving in the present, toward the future. We will also find that God speaks more, and we get to know Him more and move toward our future.

Jesus is all about reproduction: people who live like He did and who help others to do the same. Disciples who make disciples. The *'Fruit of the Spirit'*, listed in Galatians 5, is the evidence of God living in our life – changing the present. Matthew 28 is the evidence of us being a disciple of Jesus, in that we will be helping other people to become disciples of Jesus in the present time. That means that our life is changing now, so that you can offer people a better present, as well as a better future.

The best time to live as a disciple who makes disciples, is now. There will always be reasons not to, but we are here now and God knows that, so now we get to live as family on mission. If we wait for the prefect conditions, we will never do it.

Travel Toward, and Be Shaped By, the Future

> *I press on to take hold of* **that** *for which Christ Jesus took hold of me...*
>
> Philippians 3:12

You have a *'that'*! God has taken hold of you for something. The thing is, if you do not keep pressing on, you will not live in it. Living as a disciple of Jesus is not fatalism or fate, it is about us engaging with Almighty God and following Him into our future. If you do not press on, you will not take hold of that for which Jesus took hold of you. If you are a Christian, you will still spend eternity with God, but the journey there will be a disappointing, pale reflection of what it could have been.

I love the Christmas story. I sing Christmas Carols in May! Mary is a virgin who is having a baby; Jesus; God the Son. Can you imagine how that looked to Joseph? He was engaged to Mary, she tells him that she is having a baby and he knows that he hasn't slept with her and then she tells him that no one has! A lot to get your head round! Joseph himself had a dream and God spoke to him about staying with Mary and about God the Son coming to Earth.

Now events had stacked up so that Joseph had to go to Bethlehem, his ancestral home town, to register so that the government could know how many people they had and, I imagine, to make sure the taxes were being paid.

Hundreds of years before, God had said in the Bible that the Christ would be born in Bethlehem, and this was how this was going to be worked out. Joseph could have said no. He could have refused to stay with Mary or to take her with him to Bethlehem. Does that mean that Jesus would not have been born in Bethlehem and the prophecies of the Bible would have failed? Or does it mean that God would have found another way to get Mary to Bethlehem, so that Jesus would be born there, but Joseph would have missed out on being there when God showed up? I think it was the second one – which do you think?

Sometimes, travelling into the future that God has for us is hard and involves some perplexing choices, but if we will do what He says, then we will get to see Him do some amazing things in and through us. It is as we see that future by faith that we find the courage to make current choices – the future shapes the now.

As we, as King's Church, have sought to do what God has asked us to do, it has been a stretch at times for some people. There have been challenges for others, but what we are aiming to be are disciples who make disciples, not consumers who just sit back and consume: disciples produce. They help to give birth to the future.

This moves us out of our comfort zones. It makes us think, pray, fast, plan and dream. We get to press on because He has taken hold of us for much more than we have seen so far.

Jacky and I have had to learn, and are learning, that we have to press on to take hold of that for which Christ has taken hold of us – not for which other people have taken hold of us. We work this out in relationship with other people, and we are accountable to our leadership team and some close friends, but we are trying to follow Jesus.

We believe that King's is to be a missional movement, planting and growing Bases, Missional Communities and Missional Households in neighbourhoods and networks all around this area and even beyond. We want to see churches planted and international missionaries sent. We travel toward the future because we are taking seriously those words of Jesus, as He Ascended into Heaven, that our job is to be disciples of His, who make disciples.

What has God taken hold of you for? Learn from your past, be present in your present and travel toward, and live informed by, your future. Be intentional. Don't be passive. Allow your vision of the future to inform your choices in the present. Gather around you people who will share life with you and be fellow time travellers, who make the most of those *kairos* moments that can move us forward.

Chapter 15

Travelling Through the Barriers

As we move through these days, we are entering into a 'new normal'. Things have the potential to change and hopefully for the better. In recent times, we have been confronted with challenges and suffering on a global scale with the Covid 19 pandemic. We have been faced again with the evil of racism, injustice and inequality alongside massive environmental issues.

There has been a season of shaking, when things that many thought were reliable, have been shown to be insecure, but we have seen that God and His word are reliable.

It is interesting to observe that, in seasons of shaking, how some people who were in the limelight become less prominent and others step up and step forward.

In light of all this, and the brokenness and frailty of our own human condition, we know that we need a new normal.

Jesus Breaks Through Barriers

If you want to know how God feels about the barriers that divide people, then look at Jesus.

The Jews and the Samaritans hated each other. This was a long standing racial and religious issue. It's a long story, but here are the headlines. After the reign of King Solomon, hundreds of years before the events recorded in John 4 where Jesus meets and speaks to the Samaritan woman, the Hebrew people divided into two Kingdoms. The Northern Kingdom – Israel, and the Southern Kingdom – Judah. Sometimes they got on quite well and other times there was open hostility.

As their parallel, yet distinct, stories developed, (you can read them in the Bible books of Kings and Chronicles) they had times when they walked with God and times when they rebelled. Both nations, due to their rebellion to God, faced a season of exile. The Northern Kingdom was captured by enemy forces and taken into exile first and then, a little while later, the southern Kingdom.

When they returned to the land, each had a different story. The Northern Kingdom was repopulated by the world power of the day with people from other nations that they had captured and by some Hebrew people. They mixed their beliefs together somewhat and the people of the Southern Kingdom now no longer regarded them as genuine believers.

When the Southern Kingdom was restored after seventy years of exile, (you can read about this in books like Ezra, Nehemiah, Haggai and Zechariah) they regarded themselves now as the real people of God and they looked down on the Samaritans. There was both racial and religious tension for generations, yet Jesus smashed through it because He sees beyond the fixed mindsets and sees the person.

Because of the racial and religious hostility and tension that had developed between Jews and Samaritans over time, many Jews would travel around Samaria, adding miles to their journey rather than through it, but Jesus leads His disciples into Samaria.

God will not be drawn into our divisions. He stands above them and looks to break them down. In His conversation with the Samaritan woman, Jesus is going to smash through all kinds of social, racial, political and religious divides to reach a person and change a town. He is going to create the possibility of a new normal.

When people are more concerned, vocal and outraged by the damage to things than the damage that people have suffered, then we see something of the depth of the problem that we have. We need a new normal. May God give us grace, humility, courage, resolve and strength to follow the example of Jesus and break dividing walls.

May Your Kingdom come, and Your will be done on the earth as it is in Heaven

The Extra Ordinary in the Every Day

Jesus was tired and thirsty and so He sat near a well, in the heat of the day, to rest. Jesus is fully God and fully man. He is tired from the journey and rests, but in the ordinary situation of life, He is open to what His Father wants to do, and He is attentive to the Holy Spirit.

As Jesus is resting, a Samaritan woman came to draw water in middle of the day. Why? Because she was an outcast, or because she had faced rejection and pain, she could no longer deal with people. Why do I say that? Because of the words of Jesus to her,

> *The fact is, you have had five husbands, and the man you now have is not your husband. What you have just said is quite true.*
>
> John 4:18 NIV

She was either divorced, widowed or both. There were two predominant schools of thought on divorce at the time. The *Shammai* Rabbinic School, which said that the only grounds for divorce was adultery and the *Hillel* Rabbinic school, which said a man could divorce his wife for almost any reason: spoiling a meal, speaking too loudly, being disrespectful to family members. This, however, only applied to the man. A woman could only divorce her husband if he turned away from God, committed adultery or got leprosy.

These were rules made up by people, not by God. The disregard for women, in a society where a Jewish man would not speak to a Samaritan woman, is going to be smashed by Jesus because He is not defined by the misogyny of His day or the nation of His birth. He is defined by who the Father says that He is, and this sets Him free to break through barriers and to love people.

As we travel through time as disciples of Jesus, it is vital that we allow God to inform us of our identity as this sets us free to be the people that He invites us to be and to do the things that He challenges us to do.

So, this woman who meets Jesus at the well has either been rejected and divorced five times by various husbands, has been widowed five times, her husbands have been unfaithful to her five times or a mixture of the above.

This is a broken lady who has been continuously looking for security in relationships with men. She cannot face being alone and she can't deal with people. She is with a man now but not married, even though she has lived through five painful experiences of different marriages.

She knows pain and rejection. She is likely to know what it is to be the talk of the town and she wanted to socially isolate for a while. She came out at the hottest part of the day to draw water from the well, because she didn't want to see anyone. But Jesus is there alone. The disciples have gone into town to get lunch and Jesus is sat resting and thirsty.

As she walks to the well, she must have seen Jesus and expected to be ignored or maybe even insulted. However, Jesus speaks to her and asks for a drink. He invites her to do something for Him. He places Himself in her debt. She is surprised because Jesus, a Jew and a man, was speaking to her, a Samaritan and a woman. In fact, she asks,

> *The Samaritan woman said to him, 'You are a Jew and I am a Samaritan woman. How can you ask me for a drink?' (For Jews do not associate with Samaritans.)*
>
> John 4:9 NIV

Jesus crashed through the racial, social, sexist and religious barriers to connect with this human being, this woman, this person. Others would see the sexual, racial and religious divide but Jesus sees the person and He sees her need. He realises that she would not be here at this time if everything was okay. She needs a new normal.

From Religion to Relationship

They have a conversation. It begins on a very simple and everyday level, but then moves to deeper things. Jesus says,

> *... 'If you knew the gift of God and who it is that asks you for a drink, you would have asked him and he would have given you living water.'*
>
> John 4:10 NIV

At first she misses the point, but then begins to understand that He is inviting her into a new normal and she knows that she needs this and so starts to move toward it. Then, Jesus asks her to go and get her husband and she deflects from her point of pain by giving a true, but incomplete, answer – *'I have no husband,'* v17.

It is then that Jesus lets her see that He knows her pain,

> *...Jesus said to her, 'You are right when you say you have no husband. The fact is, you have had*

> *five husbands, and the man you now have is not your husband. What you have just said is quite true.'*
>
> John 4:17-18 NIV

This takes her by surprise and so she tries to shift the subject to a theological debate about where is best to worship, on the mountain in Samaria or in Jerusalem. Yet again, Jesus won't be drawn into a divisive religious debate that could well have been a smoke screen anyway. He points to a whole new reality – a new normal,

> *Yet a time is coming and has now come when the true worshipers will worship the Father in the Spirit and in truth, for they are the kind of worshipers the Father seeks. God is spirit, and his worshipers must worship in the Spirit and in truth.*
>
> John 4:23-24 NIV

God is not limited to buildings and forms. He is everywhere and He is not so much looking for our occasional acts of worship. He is looking for people who will live life as an act of worship: how they work and rest, how they treat others, how they forgive and serve, how they love, how they do family and handle money, how they keep their word and consider others, how they live as disciples who make disciples! This isn't about a building, it is a way of life in community with other followers of Jesus. Loving, serving and reaching out to those all around us; those like us and those who are different to us. This is the new normal.

As they talk, she realises that He is no ordinary person. He knows things that He could not possibly know. In fact, she becomes convinced that Jesus is the Messiah. Indeed, Jesus clearly tells her that He is!

She realises that this is no religious debate or racial rivalry. Jesus is the One who can give her a fresh start.

Friends of Jesus Tell Their Friends About Jesus

She rushes back to the village to tell people, *'Come and see a man who told me everything I ever did.'*

This lady, in all of her brokenness and pain, was a person of peace. Even though her life experiences had pushed her towards isolation, she had now encountered Jesus and there was a new normal. She was a friend of Jesus and, as the evangelist, J John says, *'Friends of Jesus tell their friends about Jesus'*.

In other places in the Gospels, Jesus talks about People of Peace. He says that they,

- Listen to you – this is what she did.
- Welcome you – she eventually does this.
- Serve you – she gives Jesus a drink.
- Introduce you to their network – she connects the whole town with Jesus. She was now the talk of the town for a very different reason.

As followers of Jesus, as we follow Him on the journey of being disciples who make disciples, we get to,

- *Humbly receive* – be interdependent. We are not developing provider/client relationships with people. Neither are we trying to sell religious services. We are inviting people into the family of God and, in a family, there is the dignity of interrelationships. We all contribute and we all benefit.

- *Share the good news* – with our words and our deeds we get to tell people about Jesus. Please don't fall for the nonsense that says, 'Preach the gospel and only if you need to use words.' You need to use words! Deeds alone are unkind because, if you really love and care about people, you will want them to meet Jesus.

> *...I am not ashamed of the gospel, because it is the power of God that brings salvation to everyone who believes...* Romans 1:16.

- *Heal what is broken* – in this case, the woman who was broken and isolated becomes the connection for the whole town to the Good News.

Jesus models this for us and, as He does, on this occasion the whole town come out to see. There was a spiritual thirst that was not initially obvious, but which was definitely there. God is already at work in the neighbourhoods and networks in which we live and move. He is already at work in the lives of those who we meet, even though they may not know it yet.

Can You See The Harvest?

At this point, the disciples return. They have been into the town that is just about to be utterly transformed by the Gospel of Jesus. Jesus says, *'Open your eyes and look at the fields! They are ripe for harvest.'* The disciples, however, were so focused on getting lunch and sorting out the shopping, that they could not see the people hungry and ready to encounter God all around them!

> *Jesus says, 'Don't you have a saying, "It's still four months until harvest"? I tell you, open your eyes and look at the fields! They are ripe for harvest. Even now the one who reaps draws a wage and harvests a crop for eternal life, so that the sower and the reaper may be glad together. Thus the saying "One sows and another reaps" is true.'*
>
> John 4:35-37 NIV

The story took place in January and, in Israel at that time, the fields would be full of people beginning to sow the corn. Jesus said to them, *'You look at the fields and think, "well, four months to harvest"'*, but He is asking them to see beyond what is obvious. As they looked across the fields, people were running from the town to hear Jesus – the harvest was ready.

The people in the town of Sychar come to faith for themselves.

> *They said to the woman, 'We no longer believe just because of what you said; now we have heard for ourselves, and we know that this man really is the Saviour of the world.'*
>
> John 4:42 NIV

The Gospel changes a town that people would not expect it to change.

Jonathan Edwards, a theologian and church leader from the 1700s, said that the task of each generation is to see the direction in which the Sovereign redeemer is moving and then to move in that direction. Will you *'lift up your eyes'* to see beyond the obvious and connect with what God is doing in His harvest field that is all around you? When is it time to sow? When is it time to water? And where and when is it time to reap a harvest?

Jesus said, *'The harvest is plentiful but the workers are few.'* There is a time under heaven for everything. In your community there will be a harvest! Where is the harvest ready at the moment? Workers are needed – will you engage with this?

Jesus is inviting us to travel to a new normal. Have you been limited and hemmed in by your preconceptions and prejudice? Is it time to follow Jesus through the limits and smallness that those things put upon us, and out into the harvest that is vast and ready?

Maybe, like the lady in our story, you feel broken, hurt, disappointed and looked down upon. Maybe you are struggling to face people. Jesus invites you to follow Him into the new normal that He has for you.

Chapter 16

Citizens of the Future Now

The over-arching story of the Bible begins in a garden with God and people together, and travels through time until it ends in a city with God and people together.

The picture of God dwelling with His people is found throughout Scripture. What does it mean for us, as God's people, to dwell with Him and one another, and for His Kingdom to come in, and through, us?

The book of Zechariah sits around the same time frame as Nehemiah, Ezra and Haggai. He was a prophet who wrote and spoke about the restoration and rebuilding of Jerusalem and the temple after the seventy year exile in Babylon. In Zechariah 8:1-5, we find some amazing verses about what it could look like to live in a city with God at the centre.

Which City Are You Living For?

As John Lennox tells us the key issue is not where you live, but where you live for. It is not the city that we live in, so much as the city that we live for, that matters. The Bible tells us that we are heading for a city that will be wonderful. The Apostle John says,

> *I saw the Holy City, the new Jerusalem, coming down out of heaven from God, prepared as a bride beautifully dressed for her husband. And I heard a loud voice from the throne saying, 'Look! God's dwelling place is now among the people, and he will dwell with them. They will be his people, and God himself will be with them and be their God. He will wipe every tear from their eyes. There will be no more death or mourning or crying or pain, for the old order of things has passed away.'*
>
> Revelation 21:2-4

If you are a follower of Jesus, that city is your home. The Apostle Paul puts it like this:

> *But our citizenship is in heaven. And we eagerly await a Saviour from there, the Lord Jesus Christ.*
>
> Philippians 3:20

So, *'our citizenship is in heaven'*. That is where we belong. That is the city that sets the culture for our lives. The norms of that city are to be our norms. How life is conducted there is to be how life is conducted in our homes and in our dealings with one another, because we are citizens of that city. However, we don't live there yet – we live here now. Here, where there is death, mourning, pain, conflict, suffering, crying, discord, etc. So, how do we get to live?

In the book of Hebrews, we read about some of the people who lived by faith. We are told of Abraham,

> *By faith he made his home in the Promised Land like a stranger in a foreign country; he lived in tents, as did Isaac and Jacob, who were heirs with him of the same promise. For he was looking*

> *forward to the city with foundations, whose architect and builder is God.*
>
> Hebrews 11:9-10

(John Lennox's book on Daniel, *Against The Flow, The Inspiration Of Daniel In An Age Of Relativism,* is an outstanding help. My thoughts in the following sections have been shaped by this book.)

How could Abraham live in the transient and challenging now? By *'looking forward to the city with foundations, whose architect and builder is God.'* He lived as a pilgrim in this land because he knew that he was a citizen of a lasting and glorious city. He sought to live by the norms and values of that city, rather than the norms and values of the world around him.

The Bible is packed full of story after story that is there to help us see how God can help us to do that. For example, Daniel was taken captive as a young man and placed in the service of the most powerful man in the world at the time. He lived in Babylon. In the Bible, that city became a sort of shorthand for a city that is set up and run for the glory of man and empowered by evil. It is the opposite of the City of God, which is set up for the glory of God and empowered by the Holy Spirit. Lennox – 'the Bible is the tale of these two cities.'

Daniel lived as a citizen of the City of God, whilst being in office and influence in the City of Babylon. How did he manage to do this? How did he manage to live right with God, and yet live in a society that was focused on the glory of man?

John Lennox says that Daniel believed that the scriptures were the word of the living God. This conviction is still the secret of how to live in 'Babylon' without 'Babylon' living in you.

There is a point, in Daniel 9, when he realised that the prophet Jeremiah had written, seventy years before, that the exile he was now in, would last for seventy years. So, Daniel sets about seeking God in prayer for Him to fulfil His Word and for the exile to end. Why? Because Daniel was so impacted by the Word of God that he really believed God had spoken to Jeremiah – perhaps that reminded him that God could speak to him too!

Do you believe that God speaks to us through the Bible? There is remarkable power in the Bible. People have given their lives so that we can have a copy of the Bible in our own language. It is valuable and powerful, but it requires us to read the Bible and to allow it to shape our thinking and our actions if it is to really have power in our lives.

The question is, 'Which city are we living for?' Are we shaped in our actions, thoughts, choices and beliefs by the Bible, or by the norms of our culture? Just because most people behave in a certain way, doesn't mean that it is right. Abraham lived as a stranger in the Promised Land. Daniel lived in Babylon, but Babylon did not live in him.

We live in a world where, increasingly, there is a disregard for God and where 'self' is seen as Lord. The one we live for is ourselves. What we want, what we need, what we think we deserve is what counts. Our comforts, our pleasures, our desires – these things are said to be first.

We live in a society that makes humans gods, and God their servant! But we are citizens of a different city!

Where do we get our views on sex from? Is it from the news, the norms of our society or from the Bible? Do we believe that sex is a good gift from God, only to be enjoyed within the boundaries of a loving marriage relationship?

What about your views on pleasure, money and time? Is the most important thing in your life that you are happy? Is your hobby more important than your Saviour? Is your money yours, or is it a gift from God? Is your home your castle, or is it an outpost of the City of God, a place of refreshing and blessing for others? These are all discipleship questions that we would encourage you to think and pray about and discuss with others.

In the story of the beginning of human history, in Genesis, the serpent seduced Adam and Eve into wanting to be like God; to rule the universe. The same lie is still being played out in 21st Century Britain. What if we really believed that God is sovereign, good, loving, kind and for people? What if we really believed that God is who we live for and not ourselves and our pleasures? What if we lived for Him instead of expecting Him to exist for us? Would the city that we live in look more like the city that is to come?

> *...the sword of the Spirit, which is the word of God.*
>
> Ephesians 6:17

God the Holy Spirit uses the word of God in our journey. Before I became a follower of Jesus I began to realise that my life needed to change. I was not brought up to go to church or read the Bible, but I began to pray and to read the Gideon Bible that I had been given some years before in school. The Holy Spirit acted like a wise doctor allowing the scriptures to give me the diagnosis of where my life was in relation to God. The Spirit used the word to help me to see my need of God. He was preparing. The first time that I ever remember hearing the gospel I was in a living room. This was months after secretly beginning to read the Bible each day. Immediately I became a follower of Jesus.

The sword of the Spirit, the word of God was used by the Holy Spirit to help to bring me to Christ and to help me to grow as a follower of Jesus. The scriptures show us how to deal with the past, live in the present in light of the future. The *'Sword of the Spirit'* (the Scriptures) come from God and point us to God. As His children we get to learn how to handle them wisely.

A Good City To Grow Up In ...A Good City To Grow Old In…

> *A Message from GOD-of-the-Angel-Armies: 'Old men and old women will come back to Jerusalem, sit on benches on the streets and spin tales, move around safely with their canes – a good city to grow old in. And boys and girls will fill the public parks, laughing and playing – a good city to grow up in.'*
>
> Zechariah 8:4-5 (*The Message*)

This, to me, is a wonderful description of God's Kingdom at work in the earth. It's a snapshot of what it can be like when we live for the city that is to come, and that city impacts and changes the villages, towns and cities, where we now live, for the better.

As we read the story of the Bible, we see that God has always wanted a visible representation of Himself, of His Kingdom in the earth. Adam and Eve failed. Old Testament Israel didn't live up to it. But, Jesus did not fail. He did live up to it – God with us. He lived in this world, as God with us, and showed us what it is like to live in the Kingdom of God; the City of God. Now we, the Church, are His Body and the Book of Ephesians says some pretty amazing things about us. Things like,

> *And God placed all things under his feet and appointed him to be head over everything for the church, which is his body, the fullness of him who fills everything in every way.*
>
> Ephesians 1:22-23

We get to be God's representatives in the earth. We get to live in the culture and norms of the City of God, in the midst of a culture that is obsessed by self and man. We get to show and tell what it is like to live for God. He intends to impact the world with His love, goodness and holiness through us. We are representatives of His city, His Kingdom here and now. We were not just saved from sin, Satan and death. We were also saved for God's purpose, here and now.

This is not all about our self-effort and striving. We get to live as citizens of the city to come, now. In the early days of King's, God gave us another scripture from the Book of Zechariah:

> *...'Jerusalem will be a city without walls because of the great number of people and animals in it. And I myself will be a wall of fire around it,' declares the LORD, 'and I will be its glory within.'*
>
> Zechariah 2:4 5

God is our protection. In Bible times, and even in later history, the city wall was very important. It set the limits of the city and served as the protection of the city. Here, God says that it is He who sets our limits and is our protection. It is so helpful if we allow that truth to really sink into our lives.

There is a difference between giving mental assent to something and really believing it. Our deeply held beliefs shape our behaviour. Does your past set the limits for your life? Do your failures and disappointments set the limits for your life? Do the opinions of others, or fear of others, set the limits for your life? Alternatively, does God set the limits? Does He get to say what is in and what is out? Does He get to say what you are capable of, or do you listen to the inner narrative that diminishes and puts you down?

Who is your protector? Your job? Your bank account? Your skills and abilities? Your connections? God?

The Gospel is Good News and, when we believe the Gospel, we are saved. Our eternal salvation is secure, but we can live in the world as if we are not following Jesus, because we are not applying the Gospel to our lives daily so that we are being saved. Let me briefly explain. According to the Bible, we as followers of Jesus have three enemies,

- The Devil – a fallen angel who opposes God and all that is good, right, loving and perfect.
- The World – not the spinning globe that we live on, or the people who live here. Rather, a system that is against the rule and reign of God. The shorthand for this, in the book of Revelation, is Babylon.
- The Flesh – or the sinful nature. That bias in us that orients itself away from God and towards self-worship, self-gratification, self-dependency, etc.

How do we overcome?

We take every thought captive: 2 Corinthians 5:10. We do not allow ourselves to have a mindset that is in opposition to what God is like and what He does and says. We are not passive, but we bring our inner beliefs and thoughts, along with the fruit of those thoughts and the actions that they produce, into submission to Christ. We put on *'the Armour of God'* (Ephesians 6) and apply the truth of the Gospel, God's Word, to our lives. We need one another to help do this. This is one of the reasons that building communities of followers of Jesus in some areas is so vital. We can help one another to remember the truth of the Gospel and to apply it to our lives.

Have you ever battled with thoughts like these?

- You really blew it this time – you should be ashamed of yourself.
- You always do stuff like that – you are such a loser.
- You will never amount to much.

They are lies and it is only as we read and apply the Bible, in the power of the Spirit, with the help and support of God's people, that we can overcome. As we do, our inner world lines up with our home in Heaven, and the world around us is changed.

As we pray, *'Let Your Kingdom come and let Your will be done on earth as it is in Heaven',* we are asking God to help us to live as citizens of Heaven here on the earth. We are asking that the manifesto of God's Kingdom would be lived out, and worked out, through us. What is that manifesto? Well, Jesus made it very clear when He read these words in the synagogue in Nazareth,

> *The Spirit of the Lord is on me, because he has anointed me to proclaim good news to the poor. He has sent me to proclaim freedom for the prisoners and recovery of sight for the blind, to set the oppressed free, to proclaim the year of the Lord's favour.*
>
> Luke 4:18-19

The more of that in the city, town or village where we live, then the place increasingly becomes, *'A good place to grow up in and a good place to grow old in.'*

We are all time travellers, moving forward one day at a time. My prayer is that we live as disciples who make disciples, so that as many people as possible will enjoy that City and our God for ever.

After this I looked, and there before me was a great multitude that no one could count, from every nation, tribe, people and language, standing before the throne and before the Lamb…

Revelation 7:9

Writers and Resources

This is our first book and over the years our thinking has been influenced and impacted by many leaders, thinkers and writers. Their wisdom has impacted us and how we approach living as disciples who make disciples. We would therefore like to acknowledge and recommend resources, podcasts and books by the following authors and speakers to help you to further explore the subjects raised in this book: Mike Breen and the 3DM Team, Tim Chester, Erwin McManus, John Lennox, Nic Harding, Phil Potter, Jeff Vanderstelt, A Hirsch, Dr R T Kendall, W Barclay, Bill Hull, Bob Rognlien, Tod Bolsinger, Francis Chan, Pete Greig, John Mark Comer, Caesar Kalinowski, Mark Sayers and Kairos Connextion (Kx).

Endings and Beginnings
P15: *Building a Discipling Culture* – Mike Breen.
Footsteps of Jesus' Pilgrimage with Bob and Pam Rognlien helped us to see some of the insights from the life of Jesus in this chapter and others.

Dressed Stones
The Challenge of Cell Church – Phil Potter

Who Gets To Join In?
Victorious Christian Service – Alan Redpath
Nehemiah Builder of Walls Leader of Men – Glenn Johnson
Building a Discipling Culture – Mike Breen
The Challenge of Cell Church – Phil Potter
5Q – Alan Hirsch
The Permanent Revolution – Alan Hirsch and Tim Catchim

Do What You Know
'Family on Mission' is a term that originates with Mike and Sally Breen
The Challenge of Cell Church – Phil Potter
Building a Discipling Culture – Mike Breen

May You Be Covered With The Dust Of Your Rabbi – Rob Bell
'Dust' Nooma DVD

Travelling Companions
Simply Christian – NT Wright
Building a Discipling Culture – Mike Breen
From Holy Laughter To Holy Fire – Michael L Brown
The Great Divorce – CS Lewis

The Journey Inside And Out
Joel Comiskey's Phd
Spiritual Depression – Dr Martyn Lloyd Jones
Transformed – Caesar Kalinowski
The Stand – song by *Hillsong*

Seeds of the Future
Information, Imitation, Innovation – Multiplying Missional Leaders – Mike Breen
Leading Missional Communities – Mike Breen and the 3DM Team
Building a Discipling Culture – Mike Breen
Leading Kingdom Movements – Mike Breen
P86-87 – focus on relationship and resources learned from Paul Maconochie in huddle context.
Transforming Leaders Into Progress Makers – Clampitt and DeKoch

Leading – Better Together
Saturate and *Gospel Fluency* – Jeff Vanderstelt
Multiplying Missional Leaders – Mike Breen
Small Is Big, Slow Is Fast – Caesar Kalinowski
Building a discipling culture – Mike Breen
Leaders Weekend structure learned from 'Kairos Connextion'

Have You Got Rhythm?
Leading Missional Communities and *Building a Discipling Culture* – Mike Breen
Family On Mission – Mike And Sally Breen

A Meal With Jesus – Tim Chester
The Gospel Primer and *Lifeschool Podcast* – Caesar Kalinowski
Reimagine Church – Nic Harding

We're Going to Need a Bigger Boat
Recovering The Past, Celtic And Roman Mission – John Finney
The Celtic Way of Evangelism – George E Hunter III
Leading Kingdom Movements – Mike Breen

Gospel-ing
The Gospel Primer and *Transformed* – Caesar Kalinowski
Gospel Fluency – Jeff Vanderstelt
You Can Change – Tim Chester
The Story Formed Way
Conversion and Discipleship: You Can't Have One Without The Other – Bill Hull
Multiplying Missional Leaders – Mike Breen

Direction of Travel
Dirty Glory – Peter Greig
The Forgotten Ways – Alan Hirsch

Travelling Through The Barriers
Building a Discipling Culture – Mike Breen
The Gospel of Luke – William Barclay

Citizens of the Future Now
Against The Flow. The Inspiration of Daniel In An Age Of Relativism – John Lennox
You Can Change – Tim Chester